With
And
Without
You

KELSEY PARKER

With And Without You

mB
MIRROR BOOKS

MIRROR BOOKS

Copyright © Kelsey Parker 2023.

The right of Kelsey Parker to be identified as the owners of this work has been asserted in accordance with the Copyright, Designs and Patents Act, 1988.

All Rights Reserved. No part of this publication may be reproduced, stored in a retrieval system, or transmitted in any form, or by any means, electronic, mechanical, photocopying, recording or otherwise without the prior permission in writing of the copyright holders, nor be otherwise circulated in any form of binding or cover other than in which it is published and without a similar condition being imposed on the subsequent publisher.

1

First published in hardback in Great Britain and Ireland in 2023 by Mirror Books, a Reach PLC business.

www.mirrorbooks.co.uk
@TheMirrorBooks

ISBN: 9781915306487
eBook ISBN: 9781915306494

Photographic acknowledgements:
Kelsey Parker personal collection, Alamy, Reach Plc.

Every effort has been made to trace copyright.
Any oversights will be rectified in future editions.

Design and production by Mirror Books.

Printed and bound by CPI Group (UK) Ltd, Croydon, CR0 4YY.

Contents

Introduction: Why? 8

1. Are You Dying? 20
2. Until We Meet Again 44
3. A New Life 64
4. Daddy's Girl 82
5. A Love Story 100
6. Dark Days of Summer 130
7. Song of Hope 158
8. Guiding Light 176
9. Stepping Out 190
10. The Greatest Gift 204
11. Gold Forever 218
12. The Future 230

Epilogue: Journey's End 260
Afterword 270
Acknowledgements 278

*Say my name like it's the last time
Live today like it's the last night
We want to cry, but we
know it's alright
'Cause I'm with you and
you're with me*

Introduction

Why?

Friday, March 10, 2023

In exactly three weeks' time, it will be a whole year since Tom died. A whole year without him gone by already. Sometimes I wonder where the time has gone — how can it be a year? Other times it feels like the longest 12 months of my life.

I miss him bouncing around the house with his broad Bolton accent, I miss his banter, I miss him playing with the kids, singing, being silly. Being Tom.

Never in a million years did I ever think that I would be a widow at 31. I mean, who does? It's the club no one

Why?

wants to ever join. Most people associate being a widow with old ladies at a cemetery with a bunch of flowers and a walking stick, I know I did. But the reality is there are so many young people out there, like me, who have lost their husbands far too soon. In fact, thousands.

I have been dreading this month arriving. As soon as the calendar hit March 1st, I just felt a total sense of dread. It is here again. The last time March was here, I was weeks away from losing the love of my life. This time last year Tom was on tour, loving being back on stage – we didn't think for one second that just weeks later he would be gone forever.

March 30th, the date Tom died, is rapidly approaching and part of me wants to slow time down. I don't want the day to come. I am not ready for it yet. I am already feeling so many emotions. Right now I am feeling anxious, I am also feeling sad, hurt, and at times, angry. I am feeling sad for the future that was taken away from Tom, the future that was robbed from us and our children. I am also feeling heartbroken that our babies will never really know their dad. Aurelia has started to ask me questions.

'Where is my daddy?' she says. 'Why don't I have a daddy?' My heart just breaks for her but what can I say? I can't lie to her. Daddy is with the angels and isn't coming home.

I am not just struggling with my emotions right now, but I feel like I have physical symptoms too. I have an annoying cough, which I am sure is a tic, and I am pretty sure it started at the beginning of the month. I think it's my anxiety presenting itself and I just can't seem to shake it.

I am also feeling guilty. Guilty that I am still here. Why did I get to stay and not Tom? Guilty that I get to see Aurelia start school this September. Guilty that I get to see Bodhi hit another milestone, say new words or bring home another picture from nursery. Guilty that we get to go on a family holiday to Greece this summer. For the past six years, Tom and I have gone camping with my mum, stepdad Johnnie, Kelsey and Dean and the children, as our families have grown. Tom used to love it. We had fresh air, everything was green, and the kids could just run, without their shoes on, and be free.

I also feel guilty for feeling so shit. After all, we are the Positive Parkers and we never let bad news or negativity bring us down. I am actually a very positive person in life. For example, I would be the one telling Tom not to read stuff on the internet that wouldn't help him or only make

Why?

him feel worse. But as the anniversary approaches I find I am struggling to feel positive every minute of the day.

I honestly wouldn't wish any of this on my worst enemy. I am not saying that for people to feel sorry for me as there is always someone worse off than you – this is something I said to Tom all the time during his illness. But I can't sugarcoat it, grief is really bloody hard.

There is no rule book when it comes to losing someone you love. People don't die and then their loved ones are given a guide on how to deal with the emotions, how to tell your children, how to sort out your finances, how to plan a funeral. There is no magical solution to dealing with the loneliness that comes at night, how to get yourself out of bed every day. If only.

There is no advice on how to deal with other people's emotions either, for example how to stop neighbours crossing the road to avoid you in the street. Yes, that's happened, but I don't blame them. What can they say? 'Sorry'. I know people are sorry. It's a sorry situation. The truth is, no one knows how to deal with death and grief, be it you going through it or your neighbour. But over the past 12 months I have had to learn and I have learned to cope in my own way.

With And Without You

Tom was such a spiritual person. He always believed that our bodies were just a temporary home for our souls, and actually it was our souls that lived forever. We actually argued over it as I disagreed with him.

'Kels there is so much more out there than this one life,' he would say.

I was very much of the belief that when you are gone, you are gone. That's it. 'Tom, don't be stupid, when you are dead, you are dead,' I'd reply.

'Trust me Kels,' he would tell me. 'We don't just have one life.'

It might sound quite deep for some people, and not everyone will hold the same beliefs, but Tom was a deep person and he really believed that your soul lives on. And now I do too.

I believe our energy is endless – it cannot be destroyed. It's a scientific fact. Albert Einstein famously said, 'Energy cannot be created or destroyed, it can only be changed from one form to another' and that's what I believe. Your energy doesn't die. It is just transferred. And our energy is our soul. Our soul is our energy.

I don't believe in coincidences and I do think everything happens for a reason – I believe in the soul journey. I believe

Why?

that when we die our souls leave our bodies and they live on forever.

Maybe Tom's soul journey was that he would only be here for 33 years but live his best life, cram in as much as possible and see the world. Life in the band took him to North America, Canada and Mexico – and they became the first UK boyband to get a top 5 hit in the US charts. Tom did everything he set out to do. He led an extraordinary life. He hadn't even had singing lessons, but somehow auditioned for a boy band and got in. Over a thousand people auditioned to get into The Wanted in 2009, and I think the whole process took about nine months, which is just crazy. Even crazier for Tom because in 2004, when he was 16, he had auditioned for the X Factor and got told no. He sang *Flying Without Wings* by Westlife and didn't even make the chorus. It knocked him for a bit, but nothing would keep Tom down for long.

Tom's brother Lewis was into music long before he was. He was five years older than Tom and could play the guitar – Lewis actually taught Tom a few chords. That was it for Tom, he caught the music bug and started reading books. He loved Indie music and taught himself how to play *Wonderwall* by Oasis. He loved Oasis and how they wrote their own music – it made Tom want to become a songwriter as well as a musician. Tom also loved that they were like him, just lads from the North. He looked up to them and they were a huge inspiration to him during his career – and that's why it felt right to have their album, Definitely Maybe, playing when Tom died.

Ever since Tom died he has given me signs. Even while writing this book, Tom has been here. When I wrote the chapter on his death, a rainbow came through my window and beamed down across my face, and when I wrote the chapter on our wedding day – which ironically and unintentionally was on the same day he proposed – my house alarm went off at 07.07am (more on those magic numbers later).

But the best and probably 'most Tom' sign came this week during a photoshoot with OK! magazine. Me and the kids were in Broadstairs for the shoot, a place which holds a very special place in my heart and was the place where Tom and I had our last holiday with the kids. As we posed together on the beach, a wave came crashing onto the shore. Sarah, who oversees all the shoots at the magazine, was taking some behind the scenes pictures, and when she looked back at the wave, it was perfectly formed

Why?

into a love heart. When she showed me, I was stunned, it was just beautiful. I have to say that was a pretty good one from Tom, and I really felt that in that moment he was there with us.

I am sure that over the next three weeks I will feel his presence even more and when March 30th arrives, I am sure I will get another sign. As long as it isn't the car alarm in the middle of the night again, please Tom.

On Tom's anniversary we are planning to take the children to one of his benches. Oh yes, Tom has not one but three – only Tom Parker could have three bloody benches! He has one close to his parents in Bolton, and he has one in Petts Wood where we live. The plaque reads 'Some days stay gold forever' which is a line from the band's song *Gold Forever*. Fans go on his anniversary or birthday to lay flowers, and we went there on the first Father's Day without him in 2022.

Then there is a third, secret bench that's so important to my family. It is a memory bench for all of the relatives we've lost. So my uncle, who died when I was teenager, has a plaque on it, my great-grandad and also more recently my grandad. It was a very special moment when my late grandad said he wanted Tom to join our family on the memory bench. It shows how important he was to my family.

Tom was loved by everyone and we shared him with everyone, but it is nice for the kids to have their own little place where they can go, especially as they get older.

We will also have a Jack Daniel's and Coke, Tom's favourite, I am sure. I know it will be a difficult day, and I know I am dreading it, but when it finally arrives I don't want it to be full of sadness. Tom will be up there saying, ''Ere why are you all moping around, have a drink and cheer up!' His life and all that he achieved deserves to be celebrated, and God, did he achieve a lot.

What comes next after the anniversary, who knows? Part of me thinks it will only get harder.

As I look back on my year of 'firsts', the first Father's day without him, his birthday, the first Christmas, each one hard for their own reasons, I worry the 'novelty' of a first won't be there any more and that fills me with dread.

One thing I am certain of though, is that I will continue where Tom left off. I will use the platform he has given me to raise more awareness of brain tumours, and I will fight for better treatments and more research into alternative therapies. I will continue to help others going through the

Why?

same thing, and not just the same cancer, but any kind of illness or trauma.

And that's why I am writing this book. I am not a grief expert or a doctor by any means, but I am a young woman who has lost the love of her life and I have a lived experience of love and loss, and I want to put that to good use to help other people.

If mine and Tom's story can help one person feel an ounce better about their situation, be it while ill or grieving themselves, then I feel like I have achieved something. I truly believe there is a reason Tom and I were soulmates, and this is it.

MARCH 2022

30th Together until the end

1

Are You Dying?

'Follow the light, Tom. If you can see a light, just follow it'

Wednesday, March 30, 2022

What can I say? My world has fallen apart. The love of my life, my best friend, has died. Tom fought so bloody hard, but in the end, his soul was ready to go.

When I die, I want a death just like Tom's. I know that might sound strange to some people, but his death was so magical. There was something so peaceful about the moment Tom passed that has made me no longer scared of dying.

Let's face it, we have all thought about dying at some point in our lives and it's terrifying. We don't want to leave our loved ones behind, especially our children, and sometimes I think that the younger they are the more fearful you are about dying and leaving them. Will they remember

Are You Dying?

me when they grow up, will they remember how much I loved them?

Then there is death itself. What will it feel like? Will it hurt? Will I know I am dying? What will happen to my body? Which is silly really because you are dead, but there is still that thought of being buried or cremated that can feel unsettling.

Tom and I never discussed death. We never discussed him dying. In fact, even when I knew he only had days left we never spoke about it. He knew, I knew, but nothing was said.

The truth is that despite Tom's tumour and its slim survival rates, we never actually thought he'd die. I know some people might think we were unrealistic or naive not to realise his prognosis wasn't good and that he wouldn't survive, but we did believe he would beat it. Tom might have been diagnosed with a brain tumour in August 2020, but he wasn't ill.

When I say that, of course he was ill in that he was living with cancer, but for most of the time he never looked ill, and he certainly didn't act ill. He was laughing and joking until the very end. Tom ate well, he exercised, his bloods were good – apart from the scans showing us this tumour, you wouldn't think he had cancer. But then one day, everything went downhill.

Tom had been on the road with The Wanted for their Greatest Hits reunion tour just weeks earlier in March 2022, and while it was only two weeks of dates, it was clear it had taken it out of him. He was desperate to go and join the boys on stage and he didn't want to miss out, and in fairness Tom was doing so well before the tour.

I remember the Friday night he came back from their last gig in Liverpool and he was absolutely buzzing. He laid down on the sofa and he was just my usual Tom, being really funny and jokey. But then the next day when he woke up, it was like he had deteriorated. I was wondering what was wrong with him? Perhaps he was just exhausted, after all he had just been on tour and he has cancer. Maybe he pushed himself too much?

Then that Saturday night while we were at our home in Petts Wood, he got up in the middle of the night to use the toilet and he fell and hurt himself. 'Shit,' I thought, though at this point I still didn't think he was going downhill.

We were due to fly to Spain for immunotherapy. We had been there in February and it had always been the plan to go back there once the tour was over to give him another

Are You Dying?

boost, but I took one look at him and knew we would have to delay it.

'I can't take him like this,' I said to my mum the next morning. He was due to fly out with a friend and I just couldn't let him go. 'It isn't fair on him and it isn't fair on everyone else. I will have to get his strength up here and then go in a week or so,' I told her.

I could tell he was disappointed because he found the clinic a comfort, but Tom was far too weak to fly.

Later that Saturday my friend Rosie came over. She would often train Tom in the garden during his treatment to improve his mind and strength. She would do light exercises with him, like weights and cardio, all while out in the fresh air. I could see how it did him the world of good. It was important that Tom kept moving and was using his muscles. Cancer is known to cause fatigue and while you might think exercise is tiring, it actually made Tom feel more alert. It was also good for his mind – it gave him 40 minutes or so to concentrate on something else, to clear his mind and give him a focus.

'I will build him up this week and then hopefully he will be back to normal,' I told her, feeling hopeful. But at that moment Tom started coughing up stuff from his lungs and Rosie and I just looked at each other. 'I have got to get the doctor to come here,' I told her. 'She will need to fly over and do the cell therapy here.'

And that was it. I was straight on the phone to the clinic in Spain arranging for Tom's doctor to fly to London. Thankfully she agreed. I booked and paid for her flights and then headed down to K2K, the performing arts school I own with my best friend Kelsey. 'I need someone who can speak Spanish,' I told them. 'Preferably fluent.'

'I know someone,' my friend Pav said. 'She's over in CrossFit next door working out. I will go get her.'

Pav introduced me to Grace and I asked her if she could help and come with me to the airport to go and collect Tom's doctor. She immediately said yes and I breathed a sigh of relief.

Some people might think it was a bit drastic or 'extra' to fly a doctor from a specialist clinic over to England on a whim, but when you are in that situation you would do anything to make the person you love feel better. And I had to do it, I had to get those dendritic cells into Tom and then I could say I did all I could to help him. It worked for him before and I was certain it would work for him again. Tom would be back to normal again soon.

Are You Dying?

Hours later the Spanish doctor was at our house and was assessing Tom. She had a puzzled look on her face. 'What's she saying, Grace?' I asked, concerned.

'She doesn't have a clue what is wrong with him,' she said to us. 'His bloods are normal, his oxygen levels are fine. She is wondering if it might be a touch of pneumonia or a chest infection of some sort.'

We thought we should get a GP to check him over in that case and prescribe him some antibiotics so I called 111. A doctor came out to see us and even he couldn't tell us what was wrong. He didn't have a temperature, everything was bang on – it was a mystery. Knowing what came next and looking back now, I really do think that his soul was probably getting ready to leave us, but his body wasn't ready to give up. Not yet.

I called Tom's bandmate Jay and told him what was going on. 'Tom's not feeling great and no one can tell me why,' I told him. 'He's unsteady on his feet and I am struggling to lift him.'

'I am coming over,' he said to me. And with that Jay was at my door with a bag telling me and Tom he was staying.

We all sat down chatting and we were filling Jay in on our dramatic episode flying the doctor over, my dash to find a translator and how Tom had become some sort of medical marvel.

Then I couldn't stop myself. The words just fell out of my mouth.

'Are you dying?' I asked him.

'Fuck off!' Tom replied, half joking, half serious.

'Well what is this Tom? I need you to explain what this is!' I felt a bit desperate and out of control.

From day one I had been all over Tom's scan, results, bloods. I felt like I knew my stuff and was an expert, though I am sure his doctors would probably disagree! But I felt I knew everything Tom was going through, and now I was lost.

'I don't know, do I?' he said.

There was a slight sadness in his eyes that I hadn't seen before. He seemed really quiet, which was unlike him, but I do think that he was probably processing the fact that he might actually be dying, thinking about the kids, thinking about us. As I say, we never talked about Tom dying, it was never up for discussion, but at that moment, I think he maybe realised something was badly wrong. And I did too. I just had this terrible, awful, gut-wrenching feeling that he wasn't going to come out of this.

Are You Dying?

Tom didn't really improve much over the next few days. He seemed to have lost some mobility and his speech was becoming affected. He just seemed weaker than usual. His mum Noreen and dad Nigel came down to see us from their home in Bolton. They were actually due to come down anyway, but I was grateful they were there.

By the following Friday, a week after he came home from the tour, I felt like he really needed some intravenous fluids. I called our local hospice, St Christopher's, and asked if they could help, and they sent someone over to the house while I was at my mum's just around the corner from our house, and Tom was with his parents.

Apparently they gave him two options, they could arrange for a hospital bed to be delivered to our house and Tom could be cared for at home, or he could come to the hospice.

I knew what Tom was like and I knew that he would have said 'yes, take me to the hospice'. I don't believe at that moment he thought he was going there to die. I think he knew he really wasn't well and I don't doubt he had been thinking about death even though we never spoke about it. I really do believe he went to the hospice thinking they would be able to build him up and give him rehab of some sorts. He went there to get better, not to die. My stepdad Johnnie drove him to the hospice and that was the last time Johnnie saw him alive. He couldn't bring himself to go back, and I think he knew it was his last goodbye to Tom as he sobbed driving home.

When I heard of Tom's decision to go to the hospice I just broke down to my mum. 'I know this is the end,' I told her. I couldn't stop myself from crying. I was broken. Absolutely devastated. It was the first time I realised I was losing Tom and it hit me out of nowhere. It all feels like a bit of a blur.

My younger brother Maxwel, who Tom adored and vice versa, came home and saw me sobbing. Maxwel was only three when Tom came into my life, and Bobbie was five, so they don't remember life before Tom.

He certainly played the big brother role with the boys, teasing them all the time, but I would say he was also a bit of a father figure. Although, of course, they have their dad Johnnie around, Tom was that much older than them both and we would take them out for movie nights and sleepovers. Basically Tom spoilt them. If they ever wanted to do something, like go to Pizza Express or to the cinema, then we would take them.

Are You Dying?

On that Friday night, Maxwel had no idea what was going on when he walked in and saw me in tears, but he just came down and sat next to me for about half an hour. I think that he must have thought, 'Oh my God, I have never seen my sister like this before'. I couldn't speak, and even if I could, I didn't know what to say.

All I wanted to do was cry and sleep. I was exhausted. I think that 18 months of exhaustion finally hit me. I hadn't slept properly since Tom was diagnosed and it had all built up. I was up and down with the kids, researching therapies in the middle of the night. I had to get the kids to preschool, sort Tom's medication, go to work at K2K, ferry Tom to appointments, then back home to do dinner, bath and bedtime. I don't know how I did it but I did. I had to. I was on autopilot.

With Tom now in the hospice, I decided to stay at my mum's house. I felt like a coward but I couldn't face the hospice. Not yet. I called all of his friends and told him he would be there and asked them to go and see him. At that moment I just felt Tom needed his family and everyone around him. I needed to take a breather to process what was happening.

Evie, a mutual friend of ours, was one of the first people

there and they had a talk, just the two of them. She is into homoeopathy and had given Tom advice throughout his illness. They spoke a lot about the soul journey and our purpose on Earth. I believe we are all here to learn lessons and teach others lessons, and I know Tom's time here was to be a brilliant musician, but then to also raise awareness of brain tumours.

I know they also spoke about what the end of Tom's life might look like but Evie didn't tell me too much. She knew how important it was for me to stay positive for Tom.

Tom loved Evie, he called her 'a witch', a nice one, like a white witch, and I know that whatever she said to him about dying, it would have brought him comfort. I know that she asked who he wanted to be with him when the time came and where he wanted to be. Knowing Tom, he wouldn't want to be at home. He didn't want our family home to have the memory of him dying there. And I know he didn't want the kids to see him deteriorate.

That Saturday after Tom went into the hospice – March 26th – I just couldn't get out of bed. 'How can I go and see my husband in a hospice?' I thought. 'I don't think I can get up there.'

I felt like a coward. Everyone was at the hospice being

Are You Dying?

there for Tom and I was moping around at my mum's house. Somehow, from somewhere, I found the strength to go. I had to do this for Tom, he needed me.

When I got to his room, I remember looking at the door – room number seven. I wouldn't usually take any notice of numbers, but it caught my attention. I wouldn't say seven was ever a lucky number for Tom while he was here with us, but I believe it is the number he uses to send me messages now. I was born on the 7th of March, and Aurelia, his first-born weighed bang on 7lbs, so I think that's why he's chosen that number.

Since Tom died my house alarm has gone off for no reason at 07:07am and my friend Holly gave birth to her little girl Daisy who weighed 7lbs 7oz. Holly even said to me afterwards that she was so terrified to give birth, but she felt like someone was in the room with her. She really believes it was Tom. In June 2023, my other friend Sacha gave birth to her baby on the 7th. I don't believe these are coincidences. I don't believe in coincidences full stop. Everything happens for a reason, good or bad. At the hospice, opening the door to number seven filled me with fear, but now the number brings me so much comfort.

I don't know what I was expecting when I walked into

Tom's room for the first time to be honest, but I don't think I expected Tom to look so well. Of course, only Tom Parker could look amazing yet so ill. And he was lapping it up. The boys were flirting with the nurses and all sorts. You really wouldn't think he was so close to dying.

'I need to go to the toilet,' he said to me. 'Tom, they don't want you getting out of the bed,' I told him.

'Yeah I know,' he sighed. 'But I want to get up, can you help me please?' He was as determined as ever. No one was going to tell Tom he was staying in bed!

And it wasn't just his physical capabilities, his mind was still sharp too. He was laughing and joking with everyone who visited, sticking his fingers up, taking the piss. He didn't have the demeanour of a dying man. But that's what he now was.

My friend Evie pulled me to one side and placed her hand on my arm. 'I think that it will be Tuesday or Wednesday,' she said to me gently.

I swallowed hard. Evie, as I say, is a bit of a white witch. She has spiritual guides and visions and I knew what she was telling me was true.

She was due to fly to Mexico on holiday and didn't want to go, but I insisted. 'By the time I land he will be gone,' she

Are You Dying?

said. It was the reality check I needed and I felt grateful that she was so honest with me. I was faced with the truth and it meant I could start to process it. Ironically, later that day a nurse called me into a side room.

'We think he has another 72 hours or so,' she said.

'I am aware,' I told her. She looked a bit surprised but there was no time to explain. I had to call anyone who hadn't yet come to see Tom. It was time to say goodbye.

I never told Tom he was going to die. He probably knew it in his heart, after all half of south east London and Bolton combined were at the hospice to see him. But if I said those words, and he knew that I knew he was going to die, it would have broken him. And I didn't want to waste time talking about death, time was something we were running out of.

That Sunday night, after a busy day at the hospice with lots of visitors, I asked to spend the night with Tom. Just the two of us. I just wanted to have one more night with him where we could talk, laugh and cuddle.

Tom's speech wasn't brilliant by this point. He had started to slur his words a little bit and some things he said were difficult to understand. His speech hadn't completely gone but he was struggling. I think I probably did all of the talking that night. 'What an incredible journey we've been on,' I told him. 'I just want to thank you for everything. For being my husband, for giving me our children.'

I remember promising him that I would fulfil all the dreams he had for our children, for them to be whatever they wanted to be. I know he would have loved to see either of them on stage, and to follow our shared passion for singing, dancing and music. I promised Tom I would raise them with good morals, good manners and kindness, all of the values we shared, and to look after them forever.

With that, Tom took off his platinum wedding ring and placed it onto my finger. It was the most romantic thing he had ever done.

There were also some laughs – I was singing to him and he always used to take the piss out of my voice. He didn't stop on his deathbed!

I looked down at my left hand and spun Tom's ring around my finger. I took it off and placed it back onto his wedding finger and kissed him.

The next 48 hours are hard to recall in exact detail, but I remember thinking I didn't want these next couple of days to be sad. I didn't want Tom to feel like people were coming to say goodbye even if he knew it. I didn't want that for him. We played music, we laughed, Jay drew rude pictures for the nurses. It wasn't the sad scene it should have been that a man in his 30s was dying. The room was full of, well, life.

I remember asking one of the nurses what I needed to do and how I knew it was time – I haven't seen anyone die before and I needed to know what to expect in those last moments. I also sought advice from various therapists and homoeopaths who had seen Tom during his cancer to ensure his last days, hours, minutes and seconds were calm and peaceful.

It also gave me a purpose – I don't mind admitting I am quite a bossy person and I like to be in charge, and I thought, 'how else can I control this situation?' I couldn't *not* do anything. I wanted to know that I did everything I possibly could for Tom right until the very end, so I reached out to Evie, and a reiki healer we had been using called Joe.

Joe lives locally to us in Petts Wood and he was brilliant for Tom during his illness. Reiki was something we read about while researching alternative therapies and Tom, as the more spiritual of us both back then, liked the idea that reiki is energy healing. Or healing for your soul. Reiki can also be used in death as the healer can help prepare your energy to leave the body. It can help with pain, bring calm and comfort.

'How can I help him?' I asked Joe at the hospice.

'Just don't let him get stuck,' he said to me. 'When the time comes you need to guide him to the light.'

It sounds like a line from the film *Ghost*, where Patrick Swayze's character Sam dies and he walks towards the light. Some people may not believe it, but I have been told this is what happens, and if you don't make it to the light, your soul will get stuck, just like Sam's. I wasn't going to take a chance, I had to help Tom on his final journey.

On Monday, Joe helped us create a healing triangle. It is a form of meditation where you are linked to two other people, in this case Evie and Tom, and you all try to visualise the same goal — for Tom's soul not to leave us. Evie was already in Mexico by this point, and I was back at home. Joe was at the hospice with Tom and did a guided meditation with him.

Afterwards, Joe called me from outside Tom's room and told me how he had taken him on a journey, but they only got so far and he couldn't go any further with him.

'I was trying to save his soul, but you can't save a soul that doesn't want to be here,' Joe said. 'His soul has to go.'

Are You Dying?

A lump started to form in my throat and I could feel tears in my eyes. 'Tom wants to stay Kelsey,' he said to me, reacting to my silence. 'His body is fighting to stay, but his soul is ready to move on now.'

Now I am sure there will be some people reading this thinking I have lost the plot and am silly to believe in what I was being told, and that's fine. I get that people prefer medical facts and figures, and if anyone ever finds themselves in the same situation as me, I think that whatever helps you and makes you feel a tiny bit more able to cope and accept the situation you are in, then that can only be a good thing. And for me, hearing Tom was ready to go brought me huge comfort. I was still absolutely devastated, but it brought me some tiny bit of peace that Tom was ready.

By Wednesday morning, Tom was in a sleepy state. He couldn't communicate, but I am certain he was aware of all that was going on around him. People would pop in and out of his room, and the friends and family room – which we jokingly called the Green Room as a nod to Tom's showbiz career – saw more people arriving.

I remember the nurses coming in to move him in the bed to prevent sores and make him as comfortable as possible.

With And Without You

'I will take that,' I said to one of them. I carefully opened Tom's left hand and took the rose quartz crystal he was holding.

Tom and I were into crystal healing and it was something we started to explore when Tom got ill. We would have crystals everywhere at home. In the kitchen, in the living room, in our bed! And it was no different when Tom was at the hospice. I am not in any way saying they cure cancer or illness, I just want to get that straight, but I do believe crystals carry good – and negative – energy and can be a comfort to those who use them. And I don't care what Tom would say about them if he was still here today, as I know he secretly loved going to bed with crystals around his feet! Rose quartz is the crystal of love and it was the one I used during the triangle healing with Joe.

As I wrapped my fingers around the heavy pink rock, I could feel it was burning hot.

'Here you go babe,' I said to him as the nurses left the room, closing the door gently behind them, and I placed the crystal back into his left hand.

With that, his breathing started to change. I was warned this would happen and it was the sign I was looking out for. Looking back I wonder if the crystal was Tom's cue to go.

Are You Dying?

By giving the crystal back to Tom, hot with his love and energy, was I subconsciously telling him it was time now, that it was OK for him to go?

Oasis's song *Live Forever* was playing quietly in the background. It was one of his favourite songs. His breathing became rapid and heavier as the next track played, another Oasis song he loved, *Champagne Supernova.*

Someday you will find me, caught beneath the landslide, in a champagne supernova in the sky…

'Follow the light,' I whispered to him as I held onto his hand. 'Follow the light, Tom. If you can see a light just follow it,' I kissed him and told him how much I loved him and then his breathing stopped. He was gone.

He looked so peaceful, his face still full of colour, just like he was sleeping, yet his chest was no longer moving. I knew he was at peace now.

I don't think Tom was scared when he died. I think that he had made peace with it. I know there were times he was terrified of dying, certainly when he was first diagnosed, but when it came to it, I think he just accepted it.

I often think about what he might have been thinking during death. I wonder if he thought, 'Is this it? All this time I have been scared, but what was I so worried about?'

With And Without You

I had already packed Tom's bag before he died, I knew he was going and I was delaying the inevitable, so I kissed him again, I told him I loved him and I said goodbye and that's it. I never saw him again.

Tom's parents and brother, Lewis, came into the room and my mum went to break the news to the others in the Green Room. I suddenly felt I needed to get out of there. I took Tom's left hand and carefully removed the crystal, still burning hot, and his wedding ring. I then placed the ring onto my wedding finger, like Tom had a few days earlier.

With the help of Tom's manager Damien Sanders, and his family, hours after Tom died we prepared a statement that would be released to the press. We needed to let the world know Tom was now no longer with us. Damien was incredible, and took the lead on it so I didn't have to. To be honest, I don't think I would have been able to put those words together without him.

I started to put the statement into an Instagram post. Part of me wanted everyone to know, to get it out there, get it done. But then the other part of me couldn't believe what I was about to post. It didn't feel real. I never expected this moment to come so I never imagined I would have to tell people Tom wasn't here any more.

Are You Dying?

It read: 'It is with the heaviest of hearts that we confirm Tom passed away peacefully earlier today with all of his family by his side.

'Our hearts are broken. Tom was the centre of our world and we can't imagine life without his infectious smile and energetic presence.

'We are truly thankful for the outpouring of love and support and ask that we all unite to ensure Tom's light continues to shine for his beautiful children. Thank you to everyone who has supported him in his care throughout. He fought until the very end.'

But before we told anyone else, I needed to call Evie. In a daze I walked out of Tom's room and into the hospice gardens. They were beautiful and the spring flowers were starting to come out. I found a bench and sat down. I didn't cry, I think I felt numb.

As I reached into my pocket to pull out my phone, a white feather fell from the sky and onto my lap.

'Tom,' I thought. 'He has passed over. He found the light.'

APRIL 2022

20th The world says goodbye to Tom

2

Until We Meet Again

*'I feel you had a bigger plan for me.
This journey has opened my eyes to
so much, and how I see the world'*

I don't know what kind of funeral Tom wanted as it wasn't something we ever discussed. We didn't consider Tom dying so why would we talk about his funeral? I know some couples who have shared with each other their thoughts and ideas on what kind of funeral they would like, whether they would want a cremation or a burial, but we just didn't.

If Tom had planned his funeral, or had at least given me an idea of what music he wanted, who would carry his coffin, then for him it was going to happen, the tumour was going to kill him, and that wasn't the mindset he wanted to have. It did mean though that I had to plan the funeral myself, but Tom and I had been together for so long, I should be able to know what he'd like.

I remember getting off the phone to Evie just after Tom died and thinking I had to get organised. Looking back now, I think that keeping my mind busy kept me going in those first few days, weeks, even months. I felt like I was on autopilot and some of it still feels hazy. I walked in circles around the car park at the hospice making mental lists of things I needed to do. I walked around so much that I am surprised I didn't wear my shoes out.

After everyone had said their goodbyes to Tom, we all went for a drink at the local pub in Bromley. It wasn't one we went to often, with kids you don't get too many nights outs at the pub, but it was the closest one to the church and I needed a drink. Most people, including The Wanted boys, had decided to go home, so I went with our families and friends. I ended up getting really, really drunk. Wine, spirits, I was drinking it all. I even remember doing shots at one point. Looking back now I don't know if I thought the alcohol was going to be a release for me or would numb the pain. Maybe it was a bit of both.

My mum went home to look after the children. That morning I had told them that Daddy was going to the angels. I just knew it was going to be that day and I didn't want to hold off telling them for any longer. It was probably the hardest conversation I have ever had to have, but I knew I had to prepare them for this day in the best way I could, especially Aurelia. She was still too young to understand what death meant, but she would have felt Tom's loss physically and wondered where he was.

'I am going to the hospice to see Daddy because I have got to make sure the angels take him today,' I told Aurelia, hoping the explanation was enough for her but knowing she wouldn't fully understand what that would mean.

Then the next morning, after Tom passed, I took a deep breath and tried to hold back my tears. I had to be strong. I will never forget her sweet little face as she looked up to me, no idea what I was about to tell her, no real understanding of the great loss this will be in her life as she grows up.

I took her into my arms and I gave her a big cuddle. 'Daddy isn't here any more, darling,' I told her gently. 'He is in the sky with the angels and the butterflies.'

I had received advice from experts on how to tell the children and was always told to be as honest as possible. I had to tell them the truth that Daddy had died, but in a way that wasn't scary.

The sad fact is that as Aurelia and Bodhi get older, neither of them will remember Tom being alive, and that just breaks my heart. Of course I will tell them everything about their dad and how much he doted on them both, all of the funny stories, how we met, his time in the band, but their memories of Tom will be based on what I tell them, or pictures. They won't remember him being physically here, the cuddles, the kisses.

That is the shittest part of all of this. Tom isn't present. He isn't physically here. It's just me and the kids. And I know there are lots of people out there who are single mums or dads and I take my hat off to all of them, because it is hard. If you need a pint of milk or have an appointment at the dentist, you all have to go. People say, 'Oh, you are superwoman' or 'I don't know how you do it, you are so strong' but I had no choice in this. It wasn't like Tom and I had come to a mutual decision to split and go our separate ways, that the children could see their dad on a weekend. For us it was final, and that is something I really struggle with.

I think in those early days and weeks after Tom died, I was in shock. I was numb. I remember after he died, I kissed him on the head, packed up his things and walked out the door. I remember my mum looking at me as if to ask what I was doing and I replied, 'Well it's not like he will need any of this stuff any more.' It took a long time for the shock to wear off, probably a whole year. And wrapped up in that first year I have felt angry and guilty and low, possibly times where I was depressed. Numbness was the main thing I felt aware of being.

When I was planning Tom's funeral, I was very much in 'let's get this organised' mode. Looking back I think I was just in disbelief and that I was having some kind of out of body experience, that none of this was happening to me.

I remember making the decision early on that the children wouldn't be going to the funeral. They were far too young and it would have been too traumatic for them. Tom didn't want them to see him in his final days, so there was no way they were going to be there. Instead, the children made a picture for Tom with their handprints and I placed it on top of his coffin.

I also made the decision not to see Tom again. The last time I saw him was when I kissed him goodbye shortly after he died. I couldn't face going to see him in the funeral home. I wanted to remember Tom for Tom. I didn't want to see him in a coffin. His stylist Luan called me and asked if she could dress him for the funeral. 'I have to dress him one last time,' she said to me. He wore a black t-shirt and jeans. It was very no-nonsense, no fuss, just very rock star. It was just very Tom.

I decided the funeral would be a celebration of his life.

Until We Meet Again

I know that sounds clichéd but I didn't want it to be a day of mourning. Tom wasn't a sad person – he once said, 'If you're having a bad day, just smile, it will make you feel better' and it is something I now live by – so I didn't want his funeral to be a day where everyone felt down. He had an extraordinary life and achieved so much, it was something to applaud. Don't get me wrong, it is really shitty that a man in his 30s has died and left his wife and little kids, and of course a funeral itself is a sad occasion, but it was important to me that people remembered their happy memories of Tom, and not Tom ill or near death.

I wanted to write a eulogy, but I knew early on there was no way I would be able to do it on the day, I knew I would get myself into a state and I wanted to be strong for Tom and do him proud, so I decided to pre-record it. I asked my friend RuthAnne, a singer and songwriter, to help me as I felt like my brain was scrambled, but when it came to putting pen to paper, the words just fell out of my mind and onto the page:

'To stand up in front of everyone right now would be too painful but I want to talk about the love of my life, my Tom… So, where do I start?

With And Without You

'19-year-old me met Tom outside of a nightclub, I say met – I instantly saw him and said, 'Oh my God, I love him'. It was love at first sight, even if he didn't know it yet.

'We went into the club, tables next to each other, and he asked for my name, which I thought was weird, but he told me, 'I wanna add you on Facebook'. And the rest is history. From that moment, I told everyone – 'I want to marry Tom Parker'.

'Tom had other ideas though because he had just joined a band called The Wanted. I didn't really believe him, but little did we know, they'd go on to be one of the UK's biggest boybands.

'Tom told me he was going to be famous and wouldn't have time for a girlfriend right now, but he didn't leave me alone. We went through lots of ups and downs at the beginning as most young couples do and it all came down to Tom crying in the bathroom of another nightclub to my next-door neighbour – who Tom had no idea was my next-door neighbour! Tom was crying his eyes out saying that he'd lost the love of his life Kelsey, which then led to me getting a phone call from Tom out of the blue and he said to me, 'I am ready'.

'And it went from zero to 100.

Until We Meet Again

'Life with you Tom was never boring, we spent a lot of our first years together drinking MAHIKI dry with a lot of people who are here today. Dancing all night long, parties in our flat, and having the funniest, most irrelevant drunken fights. And let's be honest, you all loved a Kelsey and Tom drama.

'Our relationship was fiery and fast-paced because we loved each other so much. We knew how to drive each other absolutely crazy but we definitely knew how to make up. I have too many stories to tell you all – I guess I would have to write a book. But I will happily tell those stories and cherish every moment that we shared for the rest of my life.

'So many people have said to me how much you impacted and changed their lives and I saw you always giving our loved ones the best advice, being the most supportive friend, and always coming up with ideas for people to better themselves. But most of all, I feel you had a bigger plan for me. This journey has opened my eyes to so much, and how I see the world. I feel like I see the world through your eyes now.

'Tom, your energy was never-ending, your mind never turned off and your creativity was out of this world, always coming up with songs, game shows, and we all know how much you loved an invention. I bet you're gutted you never made it onto *Dragon's Den*.

'But you packed a lot into your time and you made all of our dreams come true. Marrying you was the best day of my life, we had the best day ever and you were the best husband I could ever ask for and it has been a privilege and honour to be your wife.

'I was always so proud of everything you achieved, you never took no for an answer, you stood up for what you believed in and you were always so passionate – to the point where it was slightly on the edge but somehow you always got away with it.

'You did everything with love and absolutely no malice – and full-on Bolton boy charm, which fit right in with my family. Your daily calls to my mum… I know you're going to miss her Sunday roast and arguing with Johnnie about his business and what new car he's bought.

'My family has one word for you Tom and that's 'bullshit!' – I just wanna say thank you for being the best role model for my little brothers, I know they'll always think from now on, 'What would Tom do?' That's the kind of impact you had on everyone you met. Even my bigger brother, who should have hated you because nobody likes anyone dating their sister. But you had a way of charming people and he loved you instantly.

'And we can't forget about the three best friends… Me, you and (the other) Kelsey. We were the three best friends anyone could have.

'Mostly because of you not approving anyone she dated, to the point of me asking you not to tell her your opinion of the person, because that's how much your opinion mattered. And that's how protective you were of her heart. And then there was Dean who passed the Tom test and the three best friends became four. Some might find it weird but we really did do everything together and I know you'll miss them as much as they'll miss you.

'From all our trips to Cornwall, camping, Spain to Vegas. And guys, what happens in Vegas doesn't stay in Vegas as we welcomed our little girl Aurelia Rose Parker nine months later.

'She's a chip off the old block, a diva, born to perform and she lights up every room just like her daddy. And in typical Parker, fast-paced fashion, nine months after, we fell pregnant with our little boy, who is your absolute double. We named him Bodhi because it means enlightenment, the awakening, and he truly brought light into our lives – he is one special little boy who has your cheeky little smile.

'I have no doubt that Bodhi will grow into an amazing man just like Tom, albeit in a much calmer fashion, and continue the Parker name. I promise you that I will raise them with all the values important to you and I hope I do you proud. You've done us proud, a true warrior the past 18 months.

'You didn't allow this to hold you back, you crammed everything in from writing a book, bringing The Wanted back together, a tour, a new house, and raising money and awareness. All with me by your side, nagging you.

'You've shown our children how to be brave, courageous, strong and even in our darkest days, we stayed positive. Positive Parkers forever.

'They will always know how much you loved them and let's be honest, they've got the best guardian angel guiding them through life and so have I.

'We'll carry on your legacy forever.

'I want to thank Noreen and Nige for raising Tom into the man I fell in love with and bringing him into the world because he is my world. Soulmates. That's what we are – you are my best friend but more. The one person in the world who knows me better than anyone else and who I know better than anyone. You are the one who accepted me and believed in me before anyone else did.

'And we've truly lived a thousand years in 13 years. We've had a lifetime together and I will carry you – my soulmate – until we meet again.

'Our souls are endless, I can still feel you with me now. Remember, I love you more than you can ever say.

'If love alone could have saved you, you would have lived forever. I love you, babe, from your babe.'

On the morning of Tom's funeral – April 20th – I still felt very numb. I decided against getting traditional black funeral cars in the end. There were too many of us anyway – Tom's family, my family, Kelsey and Dean – and I just didn't have the energy to work out who would go in what car, so we decided we would walk to the church behind Tom. He was carried in a black horse-drawn carriage, just like the rock star he was, to St Francis Assisi, not far from our home in south east London.

When we turned onto the road, with the church in sight, I couldn't believe how many fans had come to pay their respects. Tom would have totally loved it. There were so many flowers, one read 'Glad You Came', which sat on the lawn outside of the church. As I walked closer to the church, gripping my mum and Johnnie for support, a beam of sunlight hit my face. I knew it was Tom.

Max, Jay, Siva and Nathan carried Tom into the church as *Champagne Supernova* played on the tannoy speakers. The music was loud, but in a strange way I felt like I could hear a pin drop.

As I walked behind Tom and the boys, all I kept thinking about was what Tom would make of all of this. I just hoped it was everything he wanted. The service was beautiful and everything we could have hoped for. Through the tears, there was some laughter, and it was a celebration of Tom's life. His brother Lewis read a eulogy on behalf of their mum Noreen and dad Nigel. It read:

'As parents, we hope that our children reach and achieve all they are capable of – reaching their hopes and dreams and in some respects a tiny bit of yours. We strive for our two boys with the hope that anything is possible with the right knowledge, self-belief and application. All the things that as parents, we had to scramble for as we progressed as a family. Tom was the epitome of that optimism.

Until We Meet Again

'Coming into the world in a hurry – a two-hour labour and there he was. He was placed into a plastic crib where he promptly raised himself up by his arms to have a good nosey around the room. The crib was quite deep so that was no mean feat for a newborn.

'It was as though he could not wait to get started – no time to hang around. He stayed awake for most of his first day on earth, much to the amusement of everyone in the ward.

'As a family we have been through so many situations with Tom, good and bad. We have nothing but love and pride for not only his achievements but his positive attitude, resourcefulness and determination.

'We always see him riding on the crest of a wave – just different waves and we'll always be faithfully at his side. An amazing son and brother who we love dearly.'

Tom's bandmates Max and Siva also spoke at the funeral. They are used to performing to crowds, but this one was obviously very different, and I could see they looked choked as they walked to the front of the church.

Max started by telling everyone how he had heard Tom's voice as he carried him saying, 'It's about time because he's carried us for the past 12 years'. It made everyone laugh and Tom would have loved that joke.

'It is with deepest sadness that we are here today but I am going to try and say some things from us boys that will make you smile about Tom,' Max began.

'Tom was, and always will be, a brother to me and my bandmates. He made us smile from the start. His love for music and how he strived for success outmatched any of us.

'His feistiness outmatched anyone on the planet. He's the only member of The Wanted that has had a punch-up with every member of The Wanted. Everything he did, he did with his best intentions so even if it was a fight he always got away with it. He got away with everything because it was Tom, it was fine.'

It's true, Tom really did have fire in his belly. He was a Leo after all, and a typical Leo at that. Confident, leading from the front, likes being the centre of attention, loves a bit of drama. But also fiercely loyal and protective over those they love. Leos are also strong and brave, just like the lion that represents them, and, ironically full of life. And Tom loved life and loved to laugh, which Max made a nod to in his reading.

'I could stand here and say so much about Tom but

you'll all have your memories about him,' Max continued. 'One thing I will always remember is his laugh. He loved laughing at people, we experienced that nearly every day. All I have got to say is he left us far too early and we'll miss him so much.'

Siva spoke next and again cut the sadness in the church with a joke about Tom looking down on us all and loving the fact the church was packed and the streets were lined with fans. There were giggles from behind me. I smiled. Tom would be loving this.

Siva then took a piece of paper and started reading from it. 'The loss of someone you love is such an undefinable thing,' he said to me. 'It appears sharply in our lives and can overwhelm us with sadness. But losing someone also reveals to us how much of an important person they were, how much of an amazing man he was.

'If we were to close our eyes and remember Tom as a person, I bet all of us would come up with totally different accounts of him. One as a loving friend, husband, brother, father and son, he was all of these and so much more. I know there's one thing we can all agree on – Tom Parker was an absolute hero.

'Without even thinking, the spiky-haired northerner asks the choreographer to show him the moves. He then proceeds to march up to anyone struggling, stand beside them and show them the choreography.

'To be honest, with Tom's dancing, I don't know if he was helping them or hurting them. But he was never afraid to stand up for us, no matter the risk. We saw it the minute we met him, and I am so glad everyone got to see that bravery over these last few months.

'The world witnessed his strength. He always cared. I believe that all of it came from that big Boltonian heart of his. For those of you who knew Tom back in the day, you knew he sometimes came across as a bit tough, but that was all a ruse. He was a true softie inside and out. When that boy loved, he loved hard, and you felt it.

'We saw it when he was around his parents, he would be giving it large and then as soon as they would visit, he would turn into a puppy and be so tender with them as well as cussing them out non-stop.' Siva had nailed Tom's personality, but I just know he was up there saying, 'Alright mate, stop telling everyone I am soft!'

And then Siva looked at me as he spoke about me and the kids. A lump formed in my throat.

Until We Meet Again

'They were everything he loved about life,' he said to me. 'He wore his heart on his sleeve, and he was loved because of it. Even on stage, once the show began, we always knew we had a sure thing in our corner.

'The boy was an absolute firecracker, and his fans always got that Parker presence. That's what brought us here today and I know that's never going to leave us.'

I had decided that I didn't want to go to the crematorium after Tom's funeral, and that we would say goodbye to him at the church. I hated the idea of him going behind a curtain too, and much preferred the idea of him being driven away. It didn't seem so cold and harsh.

As his coffin was placed back into the hearse for his final journey, I walked up to him and planted a kiss on his coffin and placed a single white flower on top. My heart broke all over again in that moment.

This is it. This really is the end.

MAY 2022

25th Helping to give birth to baby Tommy

3

A New Life

'The circle of life can be both magical and heartbreaking. I helped Tom pass over and now I've helped baby Tommy enter this world'

May 1st 2022, and yesterday marked a whole month without Tom. In some ways I don't know where that month has gone, in others each day without Tom has felt long and lonely. Waking up in the morning is the hardest. I open my eyes and there is a split second where it feels painless. And then I look over to see an empty space next to me, and it feels like a tonne of bricks have landed on my chest.

It takes every bit of strength for me to get up. And then the nights are long and lonely. My mum and auntie Julie are always here, helping me bathe the kids and put them to bed, making us home-cooked meals, but even though they are here, I still feel very alone. Does that make sense? Once the children are in bed at 6.30pm, I look at the clock and count down the minutes until I can go to bed. Until I can sleep where none of this is real and none of this has happened. Where I can dream about nice things and not

A New Life

face the nightmares I do when I am awake. The nightmare that I'm now alone. Just me and the kids.

There are mornings when I just want to pull the cover back over my head and sob my heart out, but what good is that going to do? It's not good for me, it's certainly not good for my kids. I have to be strong and present for them. But that's the thing, I haven't felt present this past month. I feel like I've been floating, on autopilot, just trying to get through each day the best I can.

In the weeks following Tom's funeral, I did the best I could to keep everything normal for Rae and Bodhi. They went to nursery as usual, they went to their K2K classes, and I went to work. Some people might think I'm crazy to go back to work so soon after Tom died, and don't get me wrong I wasn't at K2K every single day. But I needed to go and be me, to be teacher Kels, the fun, singing, dancing Kels. K2K for me is home, it's a family. I often talk about how it takes a village to raise children, get families through hardship and loss, and K2K is my village without a doubt.

I wanted to forget for just an hour the pain I was going through. I wanted that moment of escapism from what had happened. Perhaps if I was at work, then I didn't have to think about Tom's funeral, think about his final weeks, his final moments. But was that selfish of me? Selfish to not think about what had happened to us? Looking back now I think it was denial. None of this felt real. I felt empty and numb. I felt like part of me had died with Tom that day. I still do in some ways. I think the first time I felt alive again was when my friend Rosie gave birth.

They say with every death comes a birth, and just four weeks after we said our final goodbyes to Tom at his funeral, I helped our friend Rosie welcome her little precious and beautiful boy into the world. Baby Tommy.

Rosie had been Tom's personal trainer, but she ended up being one of our best friends.

When Tom was diagnosed, Rosie became Tom's third wife – after me and the other Kelsey, of course. She would come and train Tom and get his strength up, but she did so much more than just be a personal trainer. She helped him with his daily needs, was an emotional support and basically a rock to us throughout his illness. She changed up his diet and made sure he ate well and that he had all the goodness in him he needed to get better.

She brought so much positivity into our lives, though there were times when she'd lose it with Tom. Their relationship was so funny to watch. They were like an old

A New Life

married couple and would butt heads and argue over silly little things. For example, they would row over milk – yes really! I remember one day she was telling Tom how lactose-free milk contains lots of sugar and how it isn't a good thing for him to be drinking – Tom was on a sugar-free diet at this point, but no, he wasn't having any of it and was arguing with her that it didn't. When I say arguing, it was never with malice, it was just so ridiculous in the end we would all start laughing.

Rosie pushed him when they were training and that's what Tom needed. In the end, Tom was able to do a two-minute headstand. I mean who would have thought that? But he did.

They both had so much love and respect for each other underneath all that hot air. So much so that when Rosie fell pregnant, Tom had a proposition for her.

'Why don't you set up the birthing pool and have your baby here?' he asked her one day. Tom was a very kind and generous person but I don't think there are too many people he'd let give birth on our living room floor.

I remember Rosie asking me to be her birthing partner and I think I might have been speechless for the first time in my life. I felt so honoured and privileged she had asked me to share something so special with her, there was no way I was going to say no.

The weeks after the funeral had been a particularly lonely time for me. As I say, I always had the support of my family and my closest friends, but it is true that after the funeral life goes on for everyone else. They are able to miss Tom and carry on. But for me, I just couldn't. Some people said, 'Oh it's hit her now she's had Tom's funeral' but I don't think it was that. I think that it hit me the day he died. I guess after the funeral I just felt a sense of emptiness. It took me a very long time, probably a year, not to wake up and turn to the other side of the bed, expecting to see Tom sleeping next to me. Instead, there was just an oily print on the headboard from his hair wax.

I still felt numb and running on autopilot, but Rosie's gesture, a gift really, gave me a sense of purpose and I was determined to be as strong and positive as I could for her.

Rosie and her partner had sadly split up before Tommy arrived, but being 'single' parents is more common than you think and I feel like it's losing its stigma.

My mum was also a single parent and a bloody brilliant one at that. After my dad walked out on us, she raised me

A New Life

and my brother Sammy on her own. My real dad didn't want me to go to performing arts school full time. He didn't think it was a serious education or career. Despite this, from the age of five I had been enrolled at Italia Conti in Chislehurst. It was an associate school to the main one in London and they had classes every Saturday. My teacher there said to my mum that I had it in me to go full time. I think my mum was quite shocked. She could see how much I loved it, but Diane Whitlock is not Kris Jenner and a momager she was not!

'I'm not sure Kelsey,' she said to me. 'What do you think?'

'Oh my God Mum, yes, I want to go to stage school. This is my dream!' I told her.

I had to audition to get a place in the main school in London and I remember I sang *The Rhythm of Life* from *Sweet Charity*. I was such a little character and can only image what people were thinking about an 11-year-old girl singing about rhythm in the bedroom and rhythm in the street!

I remember my mum getting the call to say I had got in. I was over the moon. All of my friends in Petts Wood were going to normal secondary schools and there's me telling them all 'I'm going to be getting a train to school every day and following in the footsteps of Martine McCutcheon!' I certainly had the confidence Conti required!

I loved my time there and met some amazing people, some of whom went on to have singing or acting careers such as Pixie Lott, Lee Ryan, Zara Abrahams and dancers Mark Ballas, and Derek and Julianne Hough. Looking back now, had I not gone to Conti, I don't think I would have made it through the local comprehensive. I really do believe I would have been kicked out. I didn't want to learn. I wanted to chat to my mates during class. I wanted to perform, and of course at Conti they embraced that and embraced our individuality and personalities. We never had a playground, we just had a dance studio where we would be prancing around singing.

We still had to do the learning though. At Conti, you still had to do English, Maths and your GCSEs like any other school. But performing was a huge part of your day and I loved every second of it. Being there also gave me the confidence to talk to adults, you were treated more as a grown-up than a young student. There was more respect, and in turn, you respected your teachers. If I could put my two through stage school I would. It was the best education for me, and I look back with such lovely memories and can't help but smile.

A New Life

Before I met Tom I had a few acting roles, but it's so tough out there now. I started performing at the age of three and my dream has always been to be on stage or in a drama or a film. I wanted to be a big time actress. One role I can't wait to tell the kids about when they are older is my part as a student in Harry Potter and the Prisoner of Azkaban – I was a Hufflepuff with Cedric.

Then, when I was about 22, I played Chantelle in EastEnders in 2012. It was only five episodes but for me it was absolutely massive. I was with Tom by this point, and honestly he was my biggest cheerleader in life.

'You are going to go on to bigger and better things Kels,' he told me. 'This is it, you've cracked it now with this role. You've smashed it babe.' He really was so proud of me.

Chantelle was a rough and ready girl, probably true to what I would have been like at school. I remember the first episode coming on and 'Chantelle' was trending at number one on Twitter. The social media platform was massive then, so to see it trending was crazy.

It was all down to The Wanted fans – Tom had told them I was going to be on and they all tuned in and tweeted. I remember sending a screenshot to my agent after the five episodes had finished and I said to him, 'Send this to EastEnders, I'm trending, get them to bring Chantelle back!' I don't think he did.

I remember I had a scene with Danielle Harold and Jamie Borthwick, which is crazy as they had just filmed a storyline where Danielle's character, Lola Pearce-Brown, had a glioblastoma.

It was quite difficult to watch and, if I'm honest, I didn't see too much of it. But I've read some really good things about their portrayal and that they did a lot of research into the storyline. It's amazing that EastEnders have tackled brain tumours as it gets people talking about them and raises awareness. People might watch an episode and go away and look up 'What's a glioblastoma?'

The more we talk about these cancers and make them as prominent as say breast, cervical or testicular cancer, the more people are aware of symptoms and we can get earlier diagnoses. In Tom's case an early diagnosis wouldn't have changed things for him, but there are so many different types of cancerous tumours that would benefit, and they all deserve the same attention.

I also had a couple of film roles back in the day. In 2014, I was in an action thriller film called *Abducted* playing a character called Lily, and the following year I appeared in

A New Life

Legacy, a film written by the same creator as *Abducted* called Davie Fairbanks. It was a comedy and I played a girl called Diamond – of all names!

I also starred in a mini-series called the The Interceptor. Well, one episode anyway. I loved acting but I did find it a difficult industry to get into. I felt like I was getting rejection after rejection. But typical Tom, he would be there telling me I was brilliant.

'You are amazing Kels,' he would say to me. 'There will be something else. That one wasn't meant to be.'

'Babe you are the only one who thinks I am any good,' I said, half laughing, half serious.

But then came marriage and kids and, of course, Tom's diagnosis, so acting at the moment has been put on hold, but that's not to say I wouldn't love to get back into it. Acting, singing and dancing are my passions and I'd love to do more if I can, it's just that it's so competitive out there now. There are so many talented people and auditions can be tough – I know that myself from taking Aurelia to modelling auditions. I would love to do a gritty drama or something that I can get my teeth into. Once I get my head a bit more straight and the kids are settled at school, I might look to get an acting agent and see where it takes me.

With And Without You

Thinking about what I can do with my life is hard while I'm grieving like this but anything that can deflect my thoughts down a different path has to be a good thing.

For now I've got my K2K Stars, the performing arts academy I run with my best friend Kelsey. We were only 21 and we were both working at different performing art schools and one day we just said to each other, 'What are we doing? Why are we working for other people? We can run our own performing arts school!' And so we did.

At first we started the school for fans of The Wanted and Pixie Lott, who was my friend at Conti. We charged £20 for four hours so we took deposits from people to fund a studio in Oval, in south London, right opposite the cricket ground, and it just grew.

Then we got calls from fans who wanted us to go to Manchester, so we hopped on a train and hired out a studio in Manchester and took a class there. And then Glasgow, then Dublin. I think we also took a class in Wales.

Everyone loved it as it was workshop-based, so it wasn't just about singing and doing dance routines, but we helped people with their confidence. We would sit everyone in a circle, say our name, age, and an interesting fact about ourselves – and for some 14 or 15-year-old girls that was a

A New Life

real struggle, or they couldn't give eye contact. So it was so nice for me and Kelsey to see their confidence grow.

We decided we wanted a permanent base for our school and to work with young children – build their confidence before they become that shy 14-year-old who wants to be a star but has no confidence.

We set up our school close to a rugby club in Orpington and K2K now gives young children with the same dreams we had a stepping stone, or an opportunity, to go on and become a star. It's an amazing school and the kids are great. We have kids there who have landed West End shows or scholarships at Sylvia Young.

It makes me so proud. The students and their parents have become like family to me. Some I've seen from two years old and they are now 14 years old and smashing it. They looked after me when Tom died and long before that. Tom knew a lot of the K2K families and students and, like me, had seen them grow.

Tom was always proud of the academy and the fact the other Kelsey and I had fulfilled our own dreams of running one together. Aurelia and Bodhi both come along and Aurelia already has the makings of a total star. Well, and a diva. She's a natural born performer, very much like her dad.

With And Without You

Tom would always say in his broad northern accent, 'Babe, I can't believe she can sing in tune! It's not normal, she's only two.' She definitely gets that talent from her daddy.

Bodhi, meanwhile, is just so damn cute on stage. He has such confidence for his age and I really do think he could act if he wanted to. Both of them can be anything they want to be. Focusing on their futures and how they can make the most of their talents is something Tom would want me to be doing now.

Johnnie was always a big supporter of my dreams and has always encouraged me and my brothers. It's weird that Johnnie has actually been in our lives longer than my own dad. Him and my mum have been married for over 20 years now.

When they first met they didn't want children. My mum already had me and Sammy, and Johnnie treated us like his own. But about two years after they got together, my brother Bobbie came along in 2005, then a year later in 2006, Maxwel was born.

Even though Johnnie sees me as his daughter, and he is like a dad to me, I don't actually call him dad.

To be honest it's a hard one for me. He is very much a father figure in my life and I love him loads, but I did have a

A New Life

dad once upon a time and I think that it would be weird for me to start calling Johnnie 'Dad'. I know some people are different, and I know people who call their stepdads 'Dad', but for me he is 'Johnnie' and he is fine with that.

Tom always had such a funny relationship with Johnnie. It makes me laugh to think about the two of them together, winding each other up. They would often go fishing together.

They also had a lot of 'in' jokes. Johnnie is a roofer but he also drives buses on the side. He always used to make us come out of my mum's house and wave to him as he went by and Tom thought it was hilarious.

At Tom's funeral we hired buses to take everyone to the church and to the wake. I knew Tom would find it hilarious to have double decker buses at his funeral after all the years of taking the piss out of my stepdad. We really wanted Johnnie to drive it to Tom's funeral but we couldn't get him insured. We were gutted, Tom would have been laughing up there. 'Go on Johnnie!' he would be saying.

Now, just four weeks after the funeral and eight weeks after we lost Tom, baby Tommy was ready to come into the world.

Rosie was a total warrior during labour as I knew she would be. I'll never forget the moment she gave birth.

With And Without You

'It's a boy!' I announced and then we looked at each other. We just knew. It was a gift from my Tom. As soon as they placed little Tommy in her arms, I cried tears of joy and happiness. It was such a beautiful moment and I felt so honoured to be part of it all.

Tommy Ronnie Blake arrived on May 25th, and a little bit after one o'clock in the morning Rosie posted that he was 'an angel sent by our angel'. She also said that she almost broke my fingers during the labour!

We recently celebrated Tommy's first birthday. Kelsey and I have started to run kids' parties as a package we offer at K2K and so we threw baby Tommy a Paddington themed party at our school in Orpington. It was so magical watching all of the kids together, a new generation of friends.

Rae just dotes on Tommy, she is such a little mother hen. But while we were celebrating our baby Tommy, we were also missing our big Tommy.

He would have loved to be there. He would have been entertaining the kids, dancing, signing, chasing them around. Tom was just a big kid himself.

It has been so special seeing baby Tommy grow from the moment he was born to this little walking one-year-old. It is such a precious age.

A New Life

The circle of life can be both magical and heartbreaking. In just eight weeks I helped Tom pass over and then helped baby Tommy enter this world.

JUNE 2022
19th First Father's Day without Tom

4

Daddy's Girl

'One day Rae will meet her very own prince and it breaks my heart into a million pieces that Tom won't be there to walk her down the aisle'

It's the beginning of June already and it's been just two months since Tom died. June has been another month to dread as not only is it Aurelia's birthday, but our first Father's Day without Tom too.

The last few months have been massively up and down, but I get up and get on with it for my kids. I've got to continue and I have to actually pave something for them. I am the mum now so that's it. They have lost their dad so they need me to be as strong as possible for them at the moment. I think people are like, 'Wow, I can't believe she is actually dealing with it,' but I don't really have any other choice but to deal with it.

Explaining Tom's death to the kids has been one of the most difficult things to navigate in this whole journey. The children are young, so I just had to keep it as honest and as simple as possible. But saying to a three-year-old: 'Daddy's dead, he's gone, we're never going to see him again' sounds

Daddy's Girl

so blunt. But it had to be that black and white. I had to use the right wording, Daddy's not gone to sleep, because then they might be scared to sleep. It needed to be quite black and white. Because my mum's always been straight with me. There's never been any blurred lines, and I've really always respected my mum for that. So, my mum just said, 'Be honest with them'. That's all I can do, is be honest.

I know somewhere down the line conversations with Aurelia and Bodhi are going to change, because it's going to be, 'why did that happen? Is that likely to happen to you, Mum?' There will be so many more questions – I've literally not even touched the surface yet with them, have I really? Because they're just babies. When they're eight, I'm sure it's going to be a different conversation we're going to have.

I remember when Tom and I first discussed starting a family. We had decided to try for a baby but when it came to it, let's say Tom got stagefright.

'I can't do it,' Tom said to me.

'What are you talking about?' I asked.

'It's the pressure, I can't do it!' he said to me. Then we both fell about laughing.

We were due to get married soon, and had a small

window where we were together. Tom had been touring the country in *Grease* with Louisa Lytton so wedding planning and baby making were not at the top of his agenda.

Sparing you all the details, Tom finally found his mojo but it wasn't to be. 'Not this month,' I told him when my period came.

I could tell Tom was disappointed, but not because we didn't fall that month.

'It must be my sperm count,' he said, deadly serious. 'I should get it checked.'

'Don't be so ridiculous,' I told him. 'It was our first time properly trying for a baby. It could take up to a year.'

But Tom wasn't having any of it. His next show of the tour was in Cardiff and when he got there he booked himself into the nearest fertility clinic.

When he walked in, he was greeted by a nurse. 'Oh, hi Tom, I saw you in Grease last night and I thought you were brilliant.'

Tom said he went bright red. 'Great,' he told me on the phone from the waiting room. 'I am about to go and wank in that room and that woman knows who I am and what I am doing.'

I cracked up laughing.

Daddy's Girl

'Well you will go and get your sperm count checked for no reason, Tom!' I told him. Of course, I was right and there was absolutely nothing wrong with Tom. It just didn't happen for us that month.

Months passed, we got married and Tom was about to turn 30. A few of the other boys were also turning 30, so me, Kelsey and our friend Nicole decided to take Tom, Dean and James to Vegas to celebrate. We had the best time. Me, Kels and Dean did an eight week detox before we went – Tom was interested in joining us! – and we felt the best we ever felt. We cut out sugar and ate so well, so when we got to Vegas and started drinking, we got pissed so quickly!

We really did have the best time. We gambled, we went to pool parties, we went to all the hotel buffets and stuffed our faces. The six of us just lived our best lives. Tom liked to gamble, not in a silly way, but he knew how to play all of the games unlike me. I watched him play for a bit and then I thought I would have a go. I joined him on the roulette table and to my amazement, I kept winning.

'Do you know what this game is called, babe?' I asked him.

'Roulette, Kels,' I could see he was so pissed off that I kept winning. It was making me laugh.

With And Without You

'Nope, it's called 'I win', I said, taking the piss. It was so funny. It was his competitive streak and he hated that I was winning and he wasn't. I think I walked away with about 300 (dollars) and Tom was furious. It still makes me laugh now.

And what happens in Vegas doesn't stay in Vegas because we came home pregnant! Probably because I was in the best shape and health before I went. I have always been very regular with my periods, so when I was a day late I just knew I was pregnant. I think I was about five weeks when I took the test.

Initially my pregnancy was good. Tom doted on me and my bump and I looked after myself well.

We decided we didn't want to find out the gender, so when the 20-week scan came we told the sonographer we wanted a surprise.

By the end of May, as my due date approached, I started to really swell up. Everything just blew up – my face, my hands, my legs, my ankles. I felt so huge and was in so much pain.

Tom, however, thought it would be funny to call me Princess Fiona from Shrek and would poke me, though

Daddy's Girl

when he did it left an indent I was that swollen! He was actually really sweet though and would massage my feet every night. He also put up with my snoring. I have never been a snorer but my neck was so big and swollen, I suddenly started snoring at night.

Even though it was horrific, I just thought it was all part and parcel of pregnancy – after all, you always hear of pregnant women having swollen ankles.

But at 39 weeks I had a call from the hospital asking me to go in. The day before, I had been for a check-up, had my blood pressure taken and given them my urine sample. I left the hospital assuming everything was fine but something had obviously come up.

'You have preeclampsia,' the midwife told me when I got to the hospital. I felt like I had seen so many different midwives throughout my pregnancy that no one would have noticed how swollen I had become. It turned out a student midwife was looking at my notes and noticed my blood pressure was much higher than usual.

It was now through the roof. The midwife said that I needed to be induced.

I felt crushed. I had been practising hypnobirthing and visions of how I wanted my first birth to be. I wanted a natural labour and birth, and the thought of being induced went against all of that.

'When do you think my baby will be here?' I asked the midwife. It was now Saturday night.

'Tuesday, I reckon,' she said to me. She wasn't smiling, so she obviously wasn't joking.

'Sorry, what?' I said.

'Inductions can take a long time,' she said. 'If the pessary doesn't work, we will try a drip to get your labour going, but traditionally it won't be a quick process.'

Tom and I just looked at each other as the midwife left the room.

'Listen to me,' I said to my bump, 'you are not coming on Tuesday. You need to hurry up.'

We knew we were in for the long haul so Tom went to get us some food. Luckily I had my own room – as I wasn't in active labour they kept me away from all the screaming in the labour ward – and Tom and I sat there, eating a Papa Johns pizza.

The midwife came in with the pessary and told me to get some rest.

I turned to Tom. 'You might as well go home and get some sleep too. There's no point staying here. It's going to be a long few days and you will need it.' He took my advice but within an hour Tom was back at the hospital – my labour had started. 'That talking to the baby must have helped,' Tom smiled. 'You better call my mum,' I told him. 'I don't think it will be long now.'

Suddenly I was regretting wishing my labour on. I was in so much pain and projectile vomited in the shower room.

'Don't let anyone see me like this,' I said to Tom, feeling embarrassed. This is not how I pictured labour.

My mum arrived at the hospital and I was ready to push. I remember the midwife telling me to get on my knees.

'I can't get on my knees, they are so bloody swollen,' I told her in between intense contractions.

The pain was unbearable and the gas and air was doing very little to make me feel better. I could see Tom was getting himself in a state. He took himself off to the toilet and cried his eyes out.

'What's the matter with you?' I asked. 'Why are you bloody crying? I am the one in labour.'

'I don't like seeing you in that much pain, Kels,' he said to me. Then he turned to the midwife and said, 'God, my wife is such a bitch!' But there was no time for jokes, our baby's heart rate had dropped.

'We need to take you down to theatre,' the midwife said. Tom shot me a look. He was very aware I didn't want a C-section.

'This baby just needs a little bit of assistance to come out,' the midwife added, sensing my apprehension. 'Only one of you can accompany Kelsey,' she added.

Tom turned to my mum. 'Do you want to go?' he asked her.

'No!' she said, almost laughing. 'Tom, I think that you should go and be there at the birth of your child.'

'OK, OK' he said. I could tell he was petrified. I was petrified too.

In theatre, the doctor explained they would need to use forceps to help deliver the baby.

By this point, I just wanted to meet my baby and I wanted the pain to stop. 'OK, just do anything,' I said.

At 8.30am on Sunday, June 30th, after what felt like the longest labour ever, but was actually probably only four hours, our little Aurelia Rose was born weighing 7lbs. I loved the name Rae, I always felt it was quite cool – in keeping with me and Tom thinking we are rock stars, ha ha. But I found the name Aurelia and realised we could shorten it to Rae if we wanted. Lots of our close family call her Rae

Daddy's Girl

or Rae Rae, but Aurelia means 'the golden one'. Again, I don't believe in coincidence.

Obviously when Aurelia was born we had no idea what our future would be like. We had no idea that 15 months later, Tom would be diagnosed with the worst possible cancer that anyone could get, the Terminator. But looking back, when I think of 'the golden one', it means so much more than we can ever imagine. She has let the gold light into our lives, she is our sunshine and precious. All the connotations of gold. Also, knowing Aurelia, she will probably win an Oscar or some kind of award when she is older, taking after Daddy for sure, and they are always gold!

'You have a baby girl,' the midwife said as she handed her to me. Tom started crying again.

She was beautiful, and despite being born with forceps, she didn't have a mark on her.

'She's perfect' Tom said as he planted a kiss on my forehead. I knew from that moment he would be the best daddy ever.

Tom took to fatherhood like a duck to water. I know that's a cliché but he did. He absolutely adored Aurelia, in fact I would say he was obsessed with her, and he was always cuddling and kissing her.

From the moment she was born he wanted to be with her. I remember on the ward shortly after she was born I put her down so I could get some sleep.

'I will take her,' he said to me. Tom must have been just as shattered as I was but he wanted to soak up every moment of Aurelia's first few hours.

He even went off to get her a bottle while I was asleep.

'Gah, Tom!' I said to him, 'I am breastfeeding her, why have you given her a bottle?'

I was so annoyed, but then that all melted away when he said, 'She looked a bit hungry, I thought she might like some milk.' How could I stay angry at Tom after that? He was totally smitten and it made my heart feel so full.

Tom did everything he could to be the best dad and husband. I remember struggling with feeding Aurelia at the beginning and Tom would be on Instagram, hitting up experts and asking them for advice.

'Tom can you stop messaging people about my latch and my big swollen, cracked boobs please?' I would tell him. But I knew he was just looking after me.

When Aurelia was just a week or so old, I started to feel unwell again. I looked awful, my skin was grey and my blood pressure was up again.

Daddy's Girl

Tom really looked after us both and as cheesy as it sounds, becoming a dad made me love him even more.

He was so good at it. Aurelia wasn't the easiest of babies. She cried for what felt like the first six months of her life. In true Parker style, she wanted us all to know she arrived. Noreen, Tom's mum, said he was very much the same.

Like Tom, Aurelia was very forward for a baby. I remember her being just a couple of weeks old and we were watching Wimbledon at home with Kelsey and Dean. She was snuggled up with Kelsey and I could just see her head moving from side to side, from left to right with the ball. It was unbelievable.

She was such a strong little baby. She was so tiny, but she'd stand up on us while we were holding her, pushing down with all her strength in her little legs, and she was walking long before she was one.

Despite her months of crying, Aurelia always seemed very comfortable with her surroundings. She has always seemed so grown up for her age and wise, if I can say that about an almost four-year-old.

It was like she had been here before. Tom's mum would say the same about him.

Aurelia has just turned four and in September she will be going to school. It's another huge milestone in her young little life that her daddy will miss.

I know that when she starts school more questions will come. Why hasn't she got a daddy at sports day? Where is her daddy at parents' evening? At the nativity play? At the summer fete? She won't have a daddy to walk her to school on her first day.

A few weeks after Tom had passed, I remember Aurelia feeling very confused, yet so aware. She was confused as to where Tom was, but could sense something was going on. I could tell she was unsettled.

'Where is Daddy, Mummy? Is he at an appointment?' she would say. Or she would ask, 'Has he gone back on tour?'

'No, Daddy's dead, remember darling, he is with the angels and butterflies now and we won't be seeing him again,' I would reply.

It sounds blunt and I'm sure if she was a bit older I would have handled it a bit differently. Older children often have a slightly better grasp of death after losing pets or their grandparents for example, though of course all children are different. But how do you tell an infant their daddy has gone forever and expect them to understand?

Daddy's Girl

As well as the confusion and questions, Rae had a bit of separation anxiety too. It got so bad that she would be on the toilet with my mum near her and she would be asking after me. She wanted to know where I was all of the time. I guess it's natural, I have told her that daddy has gone away but with that she is now terrified her mummy will leave her too. I was worried for a bit about her. I could see she was struggling and I didn't want her to feel like that. But I did my best to always reassure her and if I went out to the shops or to work, I would tell her when I would be back, and as soon as I walked through the door, I would give her the biggest cuddle. I still do.

The first birthday for Rae without Tom when she turned three was hard. I was still very much operating on autopilot and just trying to get through the hours of the day. Still, I tried to keep things as normal as possible for her and even though the last thing I wanted to do was throw a party, I was determined to make it special for Rae. A bit like Tom's funeral, I knew being surrounded by our family and friends would have given us all the love we needed to get through that day. And Tom would have wanted Rae to have the best birthday. After all, he loved a party.

I had every Disney princess you can think of – Elsa,

With And Without You

Cinderella and Rapunzel – all from the K2K Academy of course, as well as a mini-castle. Rae was in awe of the princesses and I remember at one point just looking at her in her ruffled pink dress and thinking, 'Tom would be gutted to have missed this.'

When Rae turned one, we threw her a little party at home. I was pregnant with Bodhi at the time and just a week before had found out we were having a boy.

'She is going to be the best big sister,' he told me as he looked at Rae in the little bright pink tutu my auntie Julie had made her and her flower crown.

As we now celebrated her turning three, and Tom wasn't here to see it, it made me think of all the other birthdays that he will miss, her sweet 16th, turning an adult at 18 – oh God, I would have loved to see Tom parent Rae when she turned 18. Also 21, 30, and so on.

The other obvious occasion that I think about is when Rae gets married. One day she will meet her very own prince and it breaks my heart into a million pieces that Tom won't be there to walk her down the aisle. But I know for certain he will be with her every step of the way. I'm sure he will also give us a few signs if he doesn't approve of her future husband too!

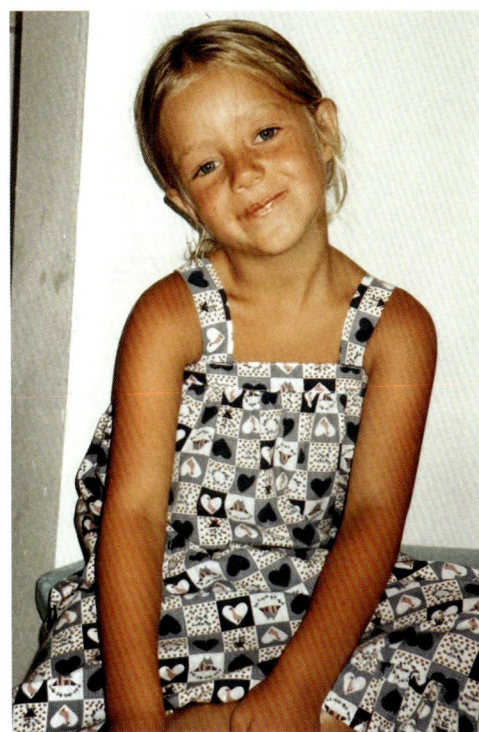

Rising star I was such a little character and can only imagine what people were thinking about an 11-year-old girl singing about rhythm in the bedroom and rhythm in the street!

All dressed up Here I am at 17 striking a pose in my bedroom. I swear this was the height of fashion at the time

Big brother Maxwel was only three when Tom came into my life, and Bobbie was five, so they don't remember life before Tom. He certainly played the big brother role, teasing them all the time

Best friend My best friend Kelsey who's been a rock for me since Tom died and helps me live out my dream of working in theatre with our K2K performing arts school

My 'village' My mum was also a single parent and a bloody brilliant one at that. After my dad left, she raised me and my brother Sammy on her own. Aunt Ju (right) has also been amazing

Capturing the moment
Dressing room antics in 2014. Every room was our studio and we took every opportunity to take pics. I'm so grateful to have so many photos of Tom for me and my kids to look back on

Where it all began
So grateful to my friend for snapping this photo of Tom chatting me up for the first time 16 years ago in Aura nightclub in Mayfair. Who would have thought that one night would change my life forever?

Young love Tom and I in 2011. Not sure I could fit any more bracelets on my wrist

Thrillseekers Ready for action on our holiday in Egypt in 2015

Couples costume Tom loved Halloween! We always made a huge effort dressing up

Our first 'child' Visit to Lulworth Cove with Dolly, our beloved dog

Drink up Cocktails with Tom in 2015 at one of our favourite bars

Smile for the camera Dolly, Tom and I on another holiday in 2016

Happiest day of my life I'm so grateful to have had the chance to marry my soulmate

I'm in a band A band? In my head I thought, 'Yeah, OK mate,' it was the oldest trick in the book. People would pretend they were footballers or actors all of the time, so I wasn't impressed by Tom's claim when we first met

Vegas baby What happens in Vegas doesn't stay in Vegas because we came home pregnant!

Always a joker Tom thought it would be funny to call me Princess Fiona from Shrek and would poke my belly

Baby Parker At 8.30am on Sunday June 30th our little Aurelia Rose was born, weighing 7lbs

Rae of sunshine
I loved the name Rae, I always felt it was quite cool – in keeping with me and Tom thinking we are rock stars, ha ha!

Daddy's Girl

I am certain that the kids can see and feel Tom. Sometimes I look at Rae or Bodhi and they are just laughing to themselves and I wonder if it's Tom. Rae talks to him all of the time. She will say 'Hello Daddy' and 'I love you Daddy'. I encourage it and say to her that she can talk to her daddy any time she wants to, when she is feeling happy or when she is sad, and that he will always be there listening.

I don't want her to be scared that he isn't here any more. I don't want my children to be sad, and neither would Tom.

JULY 2022

22nd Our wedding anniversary

5

A Love Story

'Various spiritualists and healers have said we were soulmates and our souls have been on earth together before... at the time I was blown away by our connection. It was mad'

Grief is so much bigger than I ever thought it was. There's not a box for grief. You can feel different emotions and feel things at different times, so you've just got to ride it out – that's all I can say. Sometimes in five minutes I can feel all different emotions – happy, sad, angry.

I looked back at his Instagram the other night and watched his videos that he did in lockdown. And I just miss his laugh. I miss him bouncing into a room being like, 'What's happening, babe?'

For me and Tom, we were like ultimate best friends and soulmates. We met at 19 and it was love at first sight. We shared everything and we were like the same person. People would say, 'Oh my God, you're like the boy and girl version of each other!'

'I think that I am in love – I'm going to marry that boy,' I told my friends on that fateful night nearly 16 years ago. I

A Love Story

never believed in love at first sight when I was growing up. Despite what all the Disney films say, I didn't really buy into the fact that you could just fall in love with someone there and then. That was until I met Tom.

I was on a night out with girls, including Pixie Lott and Kelsey at Aura, a nightclub in Mayfair, London and I spotted Tom in the smoking area. When we got inside, our table was next to a group of lads – Tom was one of them. It was December 2009 and even though I was only 19, I knew in that moment that Tom was the man I was going to marry.

I went up to the table and started talking to him, I was quite ballsy like that. I remember he was dressed as a proper chap and he looked like he was from London. But then he opened his mouth and this broad Bolton accent just came out and I was like, 'Ah, you are northern! I wasn't expecting that!'

'What do you do for work then?' I asked him.

'I'm in a band,' he said to me, looking well proud of himself. Tom had joined The Wanted months earlier and they were in London to create a buzz. They were having meetings, rehearsals, and getting themselves onto all the VIP tables of the best clubs in London!

I looked at Tom and just smiled. A band? In my head

I thought, 'Yeah, OK mate.' It was the oldest trick in the book. People would pretend they were footballers or actors all of the time, so I wasn't impressed by Tom's claim he was in a band.

'What's the band called then?' I asked him.

'Er, we've not got a name yet,' he said.

'Hmmm,' I thought.

But I didn't care what he did for a living. He was cute and I really fancied him.

Tom then asked me for my name. 'I am going to look you up on Facebook,' he said proudly. Apparently he thought it was a 'cool' thing to do, but I didn't! And I think my face said as much. We chatted for a bit longer, then I went back to my table to join the girls.

'He's well fit,' I told them. 'Though he reckons he is in a band,' I said, rolling my eyes.

The drinks flowed, we all danced, and the two tables – mine and Tom's – seemed to merge into one. And just when I thought that I might get a snog from him, he ended up kissing another girl who he thought was me! She was also blonde and my build, but he was so intoxicated he couldn't see she had a different face. My friend Kelsey went over and kicked him and he ended up flying into a table of drinks,

A Love Story

smashing glasses everywhere. It was a massive palaver. I was fuming. I said to him, 'You are out of order, don't talk to me again.' I still don't think he realised what was going on because apparently he went back home that night telling his mates he had kissed me!

When he woke up the next day, sobered up and realised his mistake, he tried to contact me.

He sent a text to the only Kelsey he had saved in his phone, and well, it wasn't me because he didn't take my number. The person he had text begging for forgiveness was actually a mate of his, a bloke no less, who he went to school with back home in Bolton.

Remembering he had my name, he tracked me down on Facebook. I was at work when he sent me a message a few days after that night. I was working at Dorothy Perkins in the show department and I was down in the stock room when the friend request came up.

'Gahhhhh!' I screamed to my work mate. 'It's the bloke from the other night!' I was still pissed off that he had his tongue down another girl's throat, but I was equally excited that he had messaged me.

Through Facebook I gave him my number and we were ping-ponging texts all over Christmas.

With And Without You

'It is lucky that I asked for your name for Facebook, isn't it?' Tom teased.

'Why didn't you just ask for my number and put it in your phone?' I asked.

'I thought it was a cool thing to do. I thought that's what you did in London,' he said totally seriously. 'I thought you just got people's Facebook details, not their numbers.'

Tom's pulling method was still unusual to me, but in that moment I was so glad I had a Facebook account.

'I'm coming down to London again in January,' he continued. 'We are going to launch our band.'

'Have you got a name yet?' I asked, almost teasing him.

'The Wanted,' he replied.

After that Christmas I met Tom in London. I remember feeling nervous as my train pulled into Charing Cross. Outside he was there waiting for me. He was still as fit as I remembered. Cheesy as it sounds, I loved his eyes, his smile, his tan, even the way he did his hair. Even cheesier, the first time I set eyes on Tom at Aura, I felt like he was walking in a golden light. He also had the best dress sense ever. Or so I thought. He looked like such a rock star and I loved his sense of style. That was until I found out that for our date, he had been borrowing Max's clothes, and when I finally

A Love Story

saw the contents of his wardrobe, I was like, 'Babe, we need to get you some clothes!'

Back at Charing Cross, Tom gave me a kiss and a hug. 'Alright babe,' he said. I loved Tom's accent. He just made every word sound either really calming or really funny depending whether his voice was low or high. And when Tom was funny, he was really funny. He would make me belly laugh until my ribs hurt. What I also loved about him was that he would take the piss out of himself too. He had such a great, infectious sense of humour that he wasn't afraid to rip himself.

We walked up to Nando's, the one right by the Strand, and had some food. We then walked around Covent Garden for ages and he bought me a rose. I remember when I got on the train back to Orpington thinking, 'Ahhh, I love him so much more!'

Being with Tom made me feel different than I had before. I had a few boyfriends growing up. There was a guy called Dan who, at the age of 14 I thought I had fallen in love with, but that lasted about three months. And then after that I had a guy called Joe, who had a lovely family who I got along with very well – I do feel like, as a girlfriend, I always get on well with the parents. It was probably because I was always at their houses – my house was too manic and loud with my little brothers, so I'd always be at my boyfriend's.

Next was Jordan. I met him in a nightclub – there is a theme here! – and he was so lovely. We dated for about two years after I left school and he was my first serious boyfriend. Whenever anyone sees a picture of Jordan, they say he is Tom's double. I definitely have a type!

But by September 2009, it got to a point with me and Jordan where we couldn't be together anymore. He wanted to go to London every weekend to the Ministry of Sound, and I didn't. I was quite happy to travel the world with Pixie Lott whose career was just taking off. She would have gigs in Europe and I remember Jordan had the hump one day when I flew with her to Germany. I don't know if it was jealousy, or what, but it was clear we wanted different things in life.

And then, three months after I split from Jordan, I met Tom. Again in a nightclub! The moment I set eyes on him I felt like I knew him. He felt so familiar. During Tom's journey and since he has died, various spiritualists and healers have said we were soulmates and our souls have been on earth together before, so now it makes sense, but at the time I was blown away by our connection. It was mad.

A Love Story

Back to January 2010, and our next date wasn't really a date. He was staying in a hotel in London and sharing a room with Max. He asked me to stay over with him and I obviously did. It was the first night we, well, ever did stuff. And Max was in the room. Obviously he didn't see anything but he always reminds me of it! Come on, I was 19 and we all do crazy things in the moment right?

Tom said he and his boys would be in town for a while to launch themselves. But then, I guess that's when things started to go wrong between us and we ended up going our separate ways.

Tom admitted himself he was a bit of a shit to me in that first year we were together. He put the band first and thought a girlfriend wouldn't be good for his image. You saw it a lot with boy bands back then, they all appeared single for the fans. Having a girlfriend was not something that was encouraged, let's say, because if you had one that meant you might not be popular. It all lived up to the fans' dream that the boys were single and desirable, therefore selling more singles, more albums and more gig tickets. I think One Direction broke that mould. Louis Tomlinson and his childhood sweetheart Eleanor were public from the day he won the X Factor and since then, as other boybands have come onto the scene, it is now seen as acceptable to have a girlfriend.

But not when I met Tom. He pushed me away so much that we ended up not talking for about six or seven months. I was gutted, but at the same time I wasn't going to wait around for a bloke who wasn't interested in a relationship with me. Even then at 19, I had some self-respect.

'I can't do this,' I furiously typed into my phone. I was sat at home, in my bedroom, on my own, imagining Tom getting up to all sorts in London.

'What do you mean?' he text back.

'I can't do a relationship like this,' I told him straight. 'I won't be put on the back burner while you go off and be in a band and just wait around wondering if you are coming back, so let's call it a day.' It hurt me to call things off, but no one was going to take the piss out of me.

I think he was shocked. Being in a band, he probably wasn't used to being told no. 'I want you to delete me from Facebook, my number, everything,' I said.

I know that sounds harsh, I even cringed a bit writing that, but you know what it's like. I didn't want to be the girl who was always there, the one that he could pick and put down, not saying Tom would do that, but I didn't want

A Love Story

any calls, 'Oh I am in London, come over to mine.' I didn't want to be that person. I wanted more than that, even at that young age. And you know what it is like when you are 19 and a boy pisses you right off and you become all gobby and wild, but actually inside you are heartbroken. Come on, I can't be the only one to have felt like that, ha.

And that was that. Don't get me wrong, I was really upset. And of course the band went on to be bloody massive and Tom seemed to be everywhere you looked. I was like, 'For fuck's sake, whyyy!' I think I probably played The Wanted's *All Time Low* about a million times, just torturing myself. But then, out of the blue, he texted me one day to invite me to The Wanted's first headline show at the Hammersmith Apollo in London. At first I thought, 'What a cheek, I've not heard from you in months and now you want me at your show.' But there was something telling me in my heart that I needed to go.

I think he was surprised that I actually turned up to be honest. I think I surprised myself too. Don't get me wrong, I was still pissed off with him. I went with my friend RuthAnne and the atmosphere was mad. There were thousands of screaming girls, all wearing The Wanted t-shirts, some with Tom's face on. It was very surreal. Looking back now, I don't think I really knew or took in how famous Tom actually was, or how big the band became. We couldn't go for a meal, there would be too many fans wanting a picture or an autograph. I just don't think I ever really processed how huge they were. I guess as I was there from the beginning, I went along on the ride with them, not really knowing the reaction from the 'outside', if that makes sense.

Back at the Apollo, RuthAnne said to me she could feel the chemistry between us – even though there were thousands of people at the gig. 'He keeps looking at you,' she said to me. 'It's like he is singing these songs to you.'

It's true, Tom didn't take his eyes off me the whole gig, it was like he was singing the whole concert to me. All of these fans were probably wondering, who on earth was this girl Tom keeps looking at? But I wasn't going to get away with him being a shit to me that easily. I had a game plan. My game plan was I wasn't going out after the concert – I was going home. When he invited me backstage after the gig to see the band, I said no.

'Oh, OK,' he said. 'Erm, do you want to join me and the rest of the boys in a club a bit later on. The crew are all coming, a bit of a celebration for our first gig.'

'No, sorry,' I said.

A Love Story

'Oh,' he said, looking taken aback. 'Have you got work tomorrow?'

'Nope,' I said, 'I'm just not coming.' I know it sounds harsh, but I wasn't going to give in easily.

Tom ended up going out after the gig and spent the night crying to a stranger in the bloke's toilet – only he wasn't a stranger to me, he happened to be my next door neighbour, CJ. I mean, what are the chances?

Anyway, Tom was telling CJ how he had lost the love of his life and he had made a massive mistake and CJ felt sorry for him. So much so that when I saw CJ the next morning, he told me how upset Tom was and that I should give him another chance.

'Nope,' I thought. 'He needs to try a bit harder, I'm not going to go running to him.'

And he did. Tom ended up calling me while he was away in Marbella and I remember him telling me he was 'ready'.

'Ready for what? What do you mean?' I asked him.

'I'm ready to be with you,' he said to me, all puppy dog eyes and looking sorry for himself.

'Well,' I started, 'I might not be ready to be with you!'

But I couldn't keep it up any longer. Tom had stolen my

heart and I had punished him enough. Well, almost, ha! And that is where the song RuthAnne wrote for us for Tom's proposal, *I'm Ready* came from. Some of the lyrics include, 'It was always right in front of me, I never knew'… 'I'm standing in the crowd, slowly waiting for you.'

Things became serious between us quickly. We just got each other. We were soulmates. I know it sounds clichéd but we were. He was my person, and I was his. We would know each other's minds and know how the other one was feeling or what they were thinking. I would instantly know if he was struggling, low, uncomfortable, all of those things without him even saying anything, it was almost like a sixth sense.

The boys in the band would always say that we are a boy and girl version of each other and it's so true. I can't explain the connection we had, it was mad. We had differences in that I was a bit more of a go-getter and 'get things done' person and with that I like to be in control, while Tom was a worrier and would overthink things. I'm definitely not an overthinker. But I really believe for any relationship to work you have to accept those differences. Don't get me wrong, if I could have stopped Tom worrying **about things**

A Love Story

and Googling bad shit, then yeah, that might have been nice to change. But seriously, you can't change a person and nor should you want to.

There were also so many things that we had in common. Our bond was so strong. We both loved life, we loved partying, we loved our friends and family so much. Tom wanted everyone to succeed with him, which I think is quite rare. You don't get a lot of people in life who want everybody to succeed and be the best version of themselves, but that was Tom. We are both very family-oriented people.

We also had this same understanding of trust and loyalty. All my friends would say to me, 'Only you would go out with a pop star and be OK with it.' But I was because I trusted Tom with every fibre of my being. Did I ever worry that he cheated? Absolutely not. There was a time when The Wanted cracked America and I think he spent the best part of a year over there. They had made the top 5 of the US charts in 2012, and within a year they had signed a deal with US network E! to film their own reality show, *The Wanted Life*, in Hollywood Hills. It was hard being away from Tom and I missed him but I trusted him completely. I know it wasn't always the case with some of the girlfriends over the years, and they would have concerns about them cheating, but I honestly didn't. Also, I'm not being funny, it would be quite hard for any of them to cheat on their girlfriends. Social media was taking off and if they did, I'm sure a girl would have messaged to say, 'I spent the night with him.' And knowing Tom, and the worrier he was, if a girl even went near him to flirt he would probably call me and tell me or ask what to do.

During our first few months back together, Tom was living with Jay in Wandsworth and I spent a lot of time there. It was a typical boys' pad to be honest, not that clean, but not bad enough for me not to want to stay over. I also remember Jay had a lizard that terrified me!

I love Jay's spirit, he is probably the one I vibe with the most. He is such a free person and spirit. He's the type of person that could be offered a lot of money for something huge, but if his heart isn't in it, he won't do it. He's not one to be motivated by money and fame.

I got on with all of the boys. I met Max first, as he was sharing a room with Tom when we went on our first dates in January 2010, and then I got introduced to the others. Siva also had a girlfriend, and soon Max started dating Corrie actress Michelle Keegan. I got on well with Michelle, she was such a lovely person and shier than you may think. She

A Love Story

also used to eat anything she wanted and I was always so envious as I had no idea where she put it – her figure was unreal!

After a while of staying in Wandsworth with Tom, we decided we wanted to have our own space and looked for a new apartment. I was quite happy not to stay there for much longer.

Tom and I started renting a place in Battersea which was right on the Thames. It cost a fortune, but we didn't care. It was something out of Cribs. We couldn't believe how luxurious it was with the shiny work tops and cream carpets.

We were not far from central London where we spent most nights out drinking, usually clubbing until the early hours together. Tom used to get so much free food and drink anywhere we went and as a young couple we obviously lapped it up. We thought we were absolute rock stars! We threw the most incredible parties at our place and we really did have the best time. When I look back now on that time together it makes me happy as we really did live our lives to the full. Tom was in the band, he got to travel the world, and I got to be with him. Life was so perfect.

Even at that young age, I dreamed of us having a family together. I knew early on that Tom would be the daddy to my babies. I wanted at least four children. I come from a family with three brothers. It was always so much fun growing up, though of course there were plenty of times when they would get on my nerves too. I remember our house being full of love and life and I wanted that for my children too.

I suppose that getting married wasn't as important to me as starting a family. Don't get me wrong. I wanted a nice ring and for our future children to all have the same surname, I mean who doesn't want that – but for me it was just a piece of paper. A document. It wasn't what love and a union was for me.

Tom hated it when I spoke about marriage like that, but I came from a broken home before my mum met my stepdad, and for me the real commitment was having children.

By the time I met Tom, I had no relationship with my real dad. He walked out on us six years earlier and I haven't heard from him since.

My mum and dad had met on holiday in Tenerife in the early '90s. They just got talking one day and obviously clicked from then on. I don't know too many details to be honest. It wasn't something me and my mum ever discussed, because by the time I was at an age where I should be

A Love Story

having conversations with my parents about how they got together, they had already split up.

When my mum met my dad, she already had my elder brother, Sammy, by this point. She met Sammy's dad when she was 18 and married him a year later. She knew in her gut it wasn't right and later said it was the worst decision she had ever made.

My nan had also told her not to go through with it, but being the rebel my mum is, of course she went ahead and got married anyway. However, months later they split up and she was pregnant with Sammy.

Then she met my dad. He moved in with my mum pretty much straight after they met. I think that probably at first things were OK between my mum and dad. They got married and had me, and my dad treated Sammy like his own.

But my dad had some bad habits and traits. Mum put up with a lot of shit. He would be out at the bookies, then off to the pub. I dreaded the nights he would come back from the pub. Sammy and I would sit there absolutely petrified of what mood he would be in. If he was in a bad mood, we all got punished for it.

He never ever laid a finger on me or Sammy, but he

would intimidate and scare us. He was essentially a bully and never supportive of anything we did. My mum had always been our champion, but when I said I wanted to go to performing arts school, he wasn't having any of it. He wasn't willing to spend the money on my education, or anything really, unless it was booze or gambling. He made us all so miserable and one day my mum just had enough. She filed for divorce and it all ended up in court.

I was 11 at the time and the last time I saw him was when I was on my way to school. He pulled over and I was so scared that he was going to intimidate me that I ran as fast as I could to the gates. I never saw him again. It's been nearly 20 years and there has been no contact. I am sure he's seen me in the papers or on TV and will know I married Tom, but nothing. No messages after Tom died. But I wouldn't want one – I don't need his sympathy or pity. I don't need anything from him.

Even though my mum and dad's marriage ended badly, there was never any issue with him seeing us. My mum didn't go down the route of full custody. Despite all of his faults, she wanted us to still have a relationship with our dad. I know for most of their marriage he behaved appallingly towards us, but I always think it couldn't have been all bad

A Love Story

as they were together for 13 years. And my mum would have stopped him seeing us if she felt that strongly about it. But she didn't. It was my dad's choice to walk away.

I felt sorry for Sammy because he was around 15 or 16, a shit time in a young man's life for your dad to walk out on you. And this was the second dad he had lost.

I felt quite strongly about the fact that I didn't want to have a relationship with my dad. I felt like it back then and I still feel like that today. Tom could never get his head around it. He was obsessed with the fact that I didn't want to know my dad. And when I say obsessed, he was.

Tom was known for his 'Tom tantrums'. He would fly off the handle. You would be like, 'Where did that come from?' Everyone would know about it. And me not being in contact with my biological dad really affected Tom so deeply, it was like it was his own dad. It really bothered him for hours. He came from a family where his mum and dad had a happy marriage and he hated the thought that I didn't have my dad in my life.

'You should try and find him,' he said to me, clearly frustrated. 'You've got issues.'

'I have not actually got any issues Tom,' I said. 'If you had met my dad you would know I don't want to have a relationship with him and why I don't want a person like that in my life.'

Looking back now, I wonder if Tom had such an issue with the whole dad thing because eventually his journey would mean he wouldn't be around for his own children. Deep in his subconscious did he know he would also leave his children, although under very different circumstances and not out of choice, but did he know that and did it eat away at him? It's something I often think about.

It was actually the best thing my dad did. Walking away, I mean. I don't think any man should be walking away from their kids, but in retrospect he did us all a favour. My mum went on to meet my stepdad Johnnie and my bond with Johnnie is so strong. He is such a character and supports us in all we do. He means everything to me and my brothers.

'Will you walk me down the aisle?,' I asked him amidst all the preparations for our wedding.

'Of course I will,' he said. Johnnie, the man who turned my mum's nightmare with men into a fairytale was now about to hand me over to my own prince. Like Mum, I was about to get my happy ever after.

It's now the 14th of July 2022 and it would have been our

A Love Story

four year anniversary. Many people get to celebrate four decades together, but we just had four years. But they were the best four years of our lives.

I can't say my first anniversary without Tom was hard, because I still feel like I was very numb. I don't think I felt anything. I was too empty to have feelings. I just knew I missed him. Missed him so, so much. I just wished that Tom was there, giving me a hug, making it all go away, making me feel again.

That first anniversary without him was very much a blur for me. On the day, I went for lunch with my mum, nan Linda and my auntie Ju as it was quite close to her birthday. We went to our local Turkish restaurant, Uskudar in Petts Wood, a place we all loved as a family, and my nan had bought me flowers.

Again, typical Kelsey, all I wanted to talk about was work, but this work was organising a charity day for Tom that we wanted to hold near his birthday in August. There was a lot to plan, we were having DJs, music, face painting, bouncy castles, plus a raffle, and we were expecting about 500 people. We were also going to do a walk around Petts Wood to raise money for Ahead of the Game Foundation. I love planning and organising and I think pulling together

With And Without You

that event gave me a focus on our anniversary. It gave me a sense of purpose, something I hadn't felt in a long time.

When I look at our wedding album I still can't believe I am a widow in my 30s. Since our wedding day in 2018, Tom and I have had two beautiful children and bought our family home. His diagnosis may have brought all of our future plans to an end, but I am so, so grateful for those precious years as Tom's wife.

Our wedding day was such a special day. We didn't rush to get married, Tom was in *Grease* on stage for a year, so it meant we could take our time to find the perfect venue.

One day a friend told me to check out Ridge Farm in Surrey. It was an old recording studio, which obviously Tom loved, and Queen had recorded there. On the wall there was a picture of Freddie Mercury sitting on the patio with a beer. Tom loved the musical connection and I loved that we could choose where in the venue we got married on the day. I had my heart set on getting married outside, but if it was raining there were beautiful places inside. I also loved how huge it was. We had the venue for the whole weekend and guests either stayed in the main house or in glamping tents. It was like our own little festival.

My grandad had built a stage for Tom and I to get

A Love Story

married on, and my aunt had made it all look so glamorous with chandeliers and drapes.

I remember on the night before the wedding, on the Friday, the men all got together for a drink.

'Don't go mad!' I told them. 'We are getting married tomorrow!'

But Tom did get a bit merry. It was his nerves. He has performed to massive crowds all over the world, but I would say he was the most nervous on the day we got married. In fact, he was an emotional wreck. I could see tears in his eyes as I walked down the pink aisle and he stopped to take a few deep breaths.

Johnnie walked me down the aisle and I wore a beautiful white dress by Nurit Hen Couture. It had a plunge front and cut-out sides with a full skirt. It was my dream dress, but I remember Tom freaking out when I told him the price.

'Seven grand?' he gulped.

'I am getting it for half the price,' I reassured him as he was having a mini-heart attack.

'That's still a lot of money for a dress, Kels,' he said to me, obviously not impressed by my argument that it was a bloody bargain. And then there was the bill for the music. We had The Function Band, an 8-12 piece ensemble who played a range of styles. They were brilliant but he nearly had a fit when he saw the invoice.

'It's the entertainment for the whole day,' I told him. To be fair, he might have moaned but he paid all the bills. During our interview with OK! after the wedding, Tom said the highlight for him was the band. 'The whole party atmosphere started as soon as the wedding breakfast began,' he said.

We wrote our own vows for the ceremony, which included the words, 'I take you to be my best friend, my life-long partner, I vow to help you love life, I promise I will always be there to care for you, understand you and support you.' Tom then made everyone crack up when he stumbled on the bit that read, 'I vow to share everything with you.'

RuthAnne, who was one of my eight bridesmaids, performed another song she had written for us, *The Vow*, during the ceremony and also *I'm Ready*, our engagement song, during the reception. That was followed by our first dance to *This Will Be An Everlasting Love*.

Tom was also a bit choked when he gave his speech. I won't ever forget him turning to me and saying, 'You bring me non-stop joy and happiness and laughter. I wake up every day and wonder how lucky I was to deserve you.' And

A Love Story

then, being Tom, he obviously had to finish it as a joke. 'I just wish you liked football a little bit more,' he added.

The whole wedding was full of so much love and despite being one big party like we wanted, it was actually very romantic.

Tom surprised me during a performance with Max and Jay who were ushers by inviting 18 K2K students to dance with them. He had been in secret rehearsals with them for weeks – he got me good with that one.

One thing people always say to me when we talk about our wedding day is how in love Tom and I looked. Tom and I really had a love like no other.

In the months since the funeral, a lot of people have sent me pictures of Tom and have given me stuff, but it's quite overwhelming.

There's so many beautiful pictures of him but I've put them in other places because if you have to see them everyday, that's tough. You do get teary-eyed looking at him and I think when people come round, they're choked to see them.

I've found a lot of comfort in things I didn't think I would find comfort in. I have spoken to people and they've told me we have been together in a past life and we will be together again. I massively believe that. It wasn't a coincidence I met him at 19 outside a nightclub. It was fate that brought us together and we were inseparable from the moment we met.

AUGUST 2022

4th Tom would have turned 34 this month

6

Dark Days Of Summer

'I knew at that moment that I had to be strong for Tom. He had always been strong for me and now he needed me'

It's August 2022, and five months without Tom. The days feel long, it's still light after 9pm, a time when I just want to switch off from this living hell. The nights are definitely the hardest part for me. During the day I can distract myself with the hectic day-to-day chores, looking after the kids, working, but when I wake up and I think of him, it takes me ages to get back to sleep, and it's just the constant waking up and him not being there. You can get your head around occasions like my birthday and the kids' birthdays. I can prepare myself, thinking, 'He's not going to be here.' But it could just be a casual Wednesday when I wake up and think, 'Oh my God, he's not here any more.'

It's also the month Tom would have turned 34. August 4th started as a tough day for me. Tom loved birthdays, especially his own, and I remember waking up feeling fed up. Fed up with feeling like this, fed up with the world.

But once again my K2K family were there for me, and

Dark Days Of Summer

on Tom's birthday we took the kids to see *101 Dalmations* in Regent's Park. It lifted me in a way I didn't know I needed. I think I even smiled as the kids sang *This Is Me* from *The Greatest Showman*. After all, Tom really was the greatest showman!

Three days later, we held our charity event for Tom at the Memorial Hall & Gardens in Petts Wood. It was a day I had spent the last few weeks building up to, something I could put my energy into and something to take away the loneliness and emptiness I was feeling.

We all wore blue t-shirts with Tom's picture on them and basically spent the day celebrating him and raising money for Ahead of the Game. The best thing for me was seeing my kids smile. If they are happy, I am too, and to see them smiling and celebrating Daddy was just magical for me.

Aside from Tom's birthday, August brings back darker memories. Memories I am not sure I am ready to revisit, but I know that telling Tom's complete story is something I must do. I can not hide away from the truth.

In August 2020, we had planned a break away in Norfolk with my mum, stepdad Johnnie and the rest of my family. I was six months pregnant with Bodhi at the time and we were desperate for a little family holiday with Aurelia. We had hired a huge house which overlooked the river and all we could see were fields of green.

Tom and I loved holidaying in the UK. Don't get me wrong, we were lucky enough to travel the world, especially with Tom's job. And then of course there was Thailand, America, Europe. But there is something special about holidaying at home. We love the fresh air, the scenery and the fact the kids can run around and feel the earth under their feet, otherwise known as grounding. I believe 'earthing' can bring you calm, reduce stress, pain or any inflammation. It's just a simple technique but so powerful for healing and there is no better place to earth and connect with Mother Nature than in the UK.

By this time in 2020, everyone had started to come out of lockdown and the rules had just started to relax. It felt amazing to get out, get into the car, and have a change of scenery after months of being stuck between the same four walls.

However, a month or so earlier, Tom hadn't been feeling himself. I feel terrible saying it now but I just thought he was being dramatic. He had always suffered with a bit of tinnitus, and he felt there was something wrong with his ear. Then he started to complain about having a back ache and a mark appeared on his head. I genuinely thought he had some kind of infection or virus. I wasn't that worried.

With hindsight, of course, we know that he had suffered a seizure. It happened while he was at home alone, and he couldn't really remember what had happened. I don't actually think he even knew he had a seizure. I didn't realise myself until he said he had bit through his tongue.

I thought it might be epilepsy, but didn't tell Tom that. He would have freaked out. He would have been Googling, 'Can you die from an epileptic seizure?' and all sorts, so I just kept my own thoughts to myself. I remember my friend Rosie saying to me, 'Don't tell him if you think he has had a seizure as he would worry.' She was 100 per cent right.

'If it's anything to worry about I am sure it will rear its ugly head again,' he joked. But I knew he was worried. Tom was the type of person who would worry about his health. If he had man 'flu, he would be on Google diagnosing himself with something else. Something far worse. I remember he would always have conversations with my mum where he thought he was seriously ill when it was just the sniffles. But my mum is not one of life's worriers at all, so she was the worst person to have that conversation with.

'What if it is something really bad, Di?' he would ask her.

'Well then don't worry about it because if you are ill you can't do anything about it anyway,' she would say.

People always say to me, 'Oh, you are such a strong person Kels' but my mum is exactly the same. In fact, she is far stronger than me. My mum is one of the most kind, caring and loving people you can ever meet. She has four of her own children, but Tom was like a son to her too – which is probably why she was so brutal to him with her advice! But she always gave us good advice and we would always listen to her. And the best thing about my mum is that no matter what you tell her, there is no judgement with her. In our family we always say, 'A little less judgement, a little more kindness.'

I would say my mum is very driven and knows what she wants in life. She doesn't like to follow the rules. For example, when she was younger, she would never listen to my nan and grandad. It wasn't like she was naughty, it was more that she was headstrong and thought she knew best. She has always believed she knows what is good for her and what is right – or at least she will know things feel wrong in her gut.

Tom was very close to my mum, and that's probably why he chose to tell her about his worries and fears. He felt very comfortable around her. Every Sunday we would go over there for a roast dinner if it was winter, or a barbeque if it was summer. On the rare occasion it didn't happen, Tom would feel disappointed, even offended. I think Tom did take some comfort from my mum about his seizure because she was someone he trusted and listened to, but it wasn't enough to stop him worrying completely.

I knew that the only way Tom would stop being 'Dr Google' was if he went to hospital, and if it was epilepsy, then I agreed he should be checked out.

At our local hospital, the Princess Royal in Bromley, the doctors checked Tom over and also ruled out COVID. At the time, of course, everyone coming in and out of hospital was being tested. Apart from the seizure, Tom didn't have any other symptoms, so the doctors sent him on his way satisfied that nothing was wrong.

'See, it was nothing to worry about. You've been checked over now Tom,' I reassured him. Tom still wasn't convinced. he said in his gut he knew something wasn't right. I probably sounded like the most unsympathetic wife in the world at that point... but you know what men can be like.

A week or so later, there was one episode that was really out of character for Tom and probably connected to the tumour.

With And Without You

We were in the car with my brother Maxwel and he did something. I can't even remember what it was now, but Tom just saw red and started shouting at him. I thought maybe the worry about how he was feeling was overtaking him and making him short tempered, but little did we know it was a side effect of the undiagnosed cancer.

Another red flag came when Tom said he felt concussed.

'You need to go back and tell them babe,' I told him. So Tom returned to the Princess Royal for a second time.

It was then he was offered an MRI brain scan. It was a relief for us both that he was being thoroughly checked as I knew it would put his mind at rest.

He was put on a waiting list and weeks went by. Tom still wasn't feeling 100 per cent himself, but I wouldn't say he was ill enough to cause alarm. It was more of a low mood rather than being ill. I actually thought he was feeling a bit depressed about this man 'flu or infection, or whatever it was.

He finally went for his MRI scan but we hadn't heard anything by the time we went away. 'I wonder when I will get the results,' he said to me. I could tell he was still feeling anxious.

'Babe, if the doctors thought it was an emergency, they

would have made the referral urgent,' I tried to reassure him.

I could tell he still wasn't convinced. I could see all the questions and crazy thoughts flying through his mind. 'And,' I continued, trying to stop him worrying further, 'if there was anything to worry about they would have seen it straight away and called us by now.'

I also knew that there was a huge backlog after COVID but I wasn't going to tell Tom that – I didn't want to give him more cause to feel anxious.

Despite all my reassurances, Tom's intuition was proved to be right.

It was while we were away in Norfolk that Tom suffered a huge seizure. A day earlier he had been paddle boarding along the river next to our holiday home with my cousin Reece. It made no sense to me that he could be so active and be functioning normally and then out of the blue, something like this could happen to him.

I remember the morning of the seizure. Tom had woken up – I think that we were three days or so into the holiday – and he wasn't his happy, usual self. He was moping around and it was driving me mad to be honest – we were meant to be having a nice holiday.

'For God's sake Tom,' I said. 'I can't be coping with this. You need to snap out of it.'

'I don't feel well, Kels,' he said.

'Go back to bed then,' I told him.

I feel terrible about it now, but I just thought he was being over the top. The doctors were obviously not worried, so why should we be?

But as Tom got onto the bed, he turned pale. 'Feel my hands Kels,' he said. They were pouring with sweat. It was like he had placed them both into a bowl of water.

'Lie down,' I said to him. I went to get the radio to put some music on for him and it was then that he had a massive seizure.

'Oh my God!' I screamed.

Johnnie came rushing up the stairs and took control, putting Tom into the recovery position.

Weirdly, just two days earlier, we had all been out shopping in Norfolk and Johnnie wanted some new shoes, but he was taking so long that we left him to it and went to the pub. When he came back and joined us he said that someone at the shopping centre had a seizure and he had to put them into the recovery position. Now he was helping Tom. I really do feel like it was fate that Johnnie was there with us that day.

Dark Days Of Summer

I called for an ambulance, but they were reluctant to come out. I had to argue with them to get them to come. 'Nothing like this has ever happened before,' I pleaded.

In the end they agreed to send one out. 'How long will he be in hospital for?' I asked the paramedic.

'Three or four hours, I would say,' they said. It actually ended up being three days. I wasn't allowed to go with Tom or be inside the hospital because of the COVID restrictions. It was horrendous. The longer he was in there, the more I worried. But still, I didn't think it was anything like cancer.

The doctors were really thorough and ran a series of tests on Tom – an MRI, bloods – and then I got a phone call. They said the scan showed something was up and at this point they didn't know if it was a bleed on his brain or a tumour. They said they needed to run more tests.

That's when he got the news. Tom said the doctor came to his bed and pulled the curtain around him.

'It's a brain tumour,' they told him. 'We think it is an oligodendroglioma.'

The doctor went on to explain it was a rare type of cancerous tumour, accounting for about three per cent of all tumours. 'It's a high grade tumour,' they added. 'It means it's fast growing.'

With And Without You

Recalling this makes me feel so sad, but also sick to the stomach that Tom was on his own when he was given that news. It breaks my heart that I wasn't there with him to hold his hand and tell him it was going to be OK. I can't even imagine what was going through his mind at that moment and I feel awful and guilty that he had to go through that on his own. It was a horrible shock for him to deal with by himself.

Tom said all he could say was 'Fucking hell'. Then he called me. I can't really remember too much about the conversation as it is so hazy. I remember him telling me it was definitely a tumour and not a bleed, but to be honest the rest is such a blur. I was 35 weeks pregnant at this point and had a 15-month-old baby girl and I just couldn't think straight. I think I was having some sort of out-of-body experience.

Then the doctor called me. 'I am really sorry, it's a brain tumour and I am afraid to say it's the worst-case scenario in that it's fast growing and cancerous,' they said.

I felt like the world had stopped for a second. I just froze, took in what I was being told and then it hit me. I felt like I was going to pass out. I was in a total state. The doctor went on to explain there were treatment options and he would need a biopsy for an official and formal diagnosis.

Dark Days Of Summer

I remember the words 'chemo' and radiotherapy' being mentioned but my head was spinning.

The doctor then said to me, and I will never forget this, it has always stuck with me, but he said, 'I can't tell you how long he has got left, because everybody is different. Literally everybody is different.'

I remember thinking, 'What am I going to do?' I suddenly felt a real sense of panic and I felt scared for Tom. 'I can't lose him,' I told myself. 'We are going to fight this.'

Back in London, Tom had an appointment at King's College Hospital where they did a biopsy. We knew it was a cancerous tumour from what we were told while in Norwich, but we didn't expect what was going to come next.

Rather than dealing with a possible high grade oligodendroglioma, we were told the results of the biopsy showed that it was in fact a grade four glioblastoma.

The deadliest of all brain tumours.

While those with an oligodendroglioma have a 30-40 per cent chance of surviving five or more years after being diagnosed, those with a glioblastoma, or a 'glio' as we came to call it, was far, far less. It was more like a five per cent survival rate after five years.

To be given that news was just the worst possible feeling we've ever experienced. You think you are dealing with one thing, but then you're told it's something far more sinister. It was a hell of a lot to process.

The doctors explained there were two tumours, one smaller one on the lower right side of his brain, and another bigger one on the left. It was this one that was inoperable, due to where it was sat.

'We can give you radiotherapy to try to shrink it and then we would look at chemo,' the doctor said.

The aim was a two-pronged attack to try and keep the larger one under control, and hopefully shrink the smaller one until it was gone. We were warned that new tumours could pop up, but if that happened they would just throw everything at them to try and shrink them again.

I looked at Tom and could see he was a broken man. I knew he wanted to ask how long he had left, but I stopped him.

'We don't want a prognosis,' I told the doctor. He nodded, accepting my wishes. He obviously knew what Tom's future would look like – that was between 12 to 15 months in most glioblastoma cases – but we didn't want to know how long that future would be for.

Dark Days Of Summer

Some people prefer to know how long they have left so they can get things in order or complete a bucket list. But if the doctor told Tom he had three months, then he would have sat there with a calendar crossing off the days; he wouldn't be living. He would be Googling bad stuff and getting himself into a negative mindset.

I guess it goes back to what I was saying about Tom being my soulmate – I just knew what was right for him in that moment and that he wouldn't be able to cope with or process that information. We would have lost him there and then. His mind would have gone and wouldn't have concentrated on anything else but that prognosis. And how can doctors really make a prognosis anyway? That's why they are always so broad, because no one can really pinpoint how long you have left. No one has a crystal ball that can give you an exact date. If the doctor had said 'you have between six and 18 months' then Tom would have heard six and that would have been it. Worst case scenario only.

I knew at that moment that I had to be strong for Tom. He had always been strong for me and now he needed me. As I've suggested, I like to have control of things and can sometimes be a little bit bossy – I grew up in a house of boys, a girl had to find her voice! – but Tom took care of the mortgage, the bills, anything like that. There used to be ongoing joke between us that I wouldn't make phone calls, no matter what the situation. I wouldn't even phone up for a pizza, I'd be shouting, 'Tom!!!'

He cared for me and the kids. He took care of things and was always reliable – well, most of the time, ha ha! – and Tom would say that I was his rock, even before all this, that I propped him up when he was down. Nothing could've been achieved if we didn't do it together. That's what our marriage was about. Supporting each other. Being there for each other.

So I knew deep down in my heart that if we had any chance of Tom beating this – yes, I really did think he could – then he needed to be positive every step of the way, and he had to believe he could beat it.

Not just believe it, but see it. He had to imagine himself getting through this. For me, this was now a test of mental strength as well as treatment.

Tom wanted to know his prognosis though. I remember there was one appointment I couldn't go to and his brother Lewis took him instead. I said to him, 'Don't let them tell him anything' but Lewis told me Tom spent the appointment fishing for clues.

To this day I don't regret Tom not finding out. Since

Dark Days Of Summer

Tom's death, I have spoken to his doctor, and he told me that when he first saw us after the biopsy, Tom was looking at weeks and not months. Thank God we didn't find out. I really do think it would have killed Tom, literally. He would have withdrawn inside himself and would not have fought the way he did.

Instead, oblivious to his prognosis, Tom was boosted by other people's stories. There was one bloke called Ben who was diagnosed 25 years ago and he's still with us. And then there was another bloke called Dave Bolton who was diagnosed with a glioblastoma at a similar age to Tom and he is still here 10 years later. He is in the top two per cent of glioblastoma sufferers who survive beyond 10 years. It's a very low percentage, but a two per cent chance is still a chance. It was those stories that gave us hope.

Tom was overwhelmed by the support he received from his fans, and I think that made him feel better than any drug. But he was still a changed man. I always say I lost Tom the moment he was diagnosed. As positive as he was, and no matter how strong his mind was, something changed. He never was the same Tom again. How could he be? We could throw everything we could at these tumours, but the fact we were even having to do this was just horrendous.

With And Without You

Tom was a very lost man especially in those early weeks after he was diagnosed. He struggled to get out of bed both mentally and physically. He was crushed. He wasn't just processing the fact that he had this tumour, but he was also worrying about how people saw him. Tom was a showman, a joker, he made people laugh – he didn't want people to suddenly start treating him differently just because he had cancer. I think he was probably more terrified of that than he was of the tumour itself.

'You are going to be alright you know, babe,' I told him.

I remember him asking me how I stayed so strong. I don't know how, I guess in that moment you can either crack on or crumble, and I decided on the former. I wasn't going to let this tumour destroy our future, our family – this is meant to be a happy time for us. From the beginning I knew I had to keep his spirits up and his mind clear and full of positivity.

About six weeks after Tom's diagnosis, he decided to go public with his news. It was his biggest fear – the news would be out there and everyone would know. It's in black and white. I guess there was also that anxiety that it somehow made it more real if we told people.

We knew the news would get out eventually and we

always had that fear he would be spotted or pictured at the hospital. We didn't want to take the risk. It was stressful enough as it was and we didn't want to live like that.

Around the time Tom was diagnosed, Sarah Harding revealed she had been diagnosed with breast cancer. It was such a shock. Like Tom, she was so young. And she was also a close friend after she appeared on The Jump with Tom. What are the chances of two people from the same reality show being diagnosed with cancer in their 30s?

Sarah publicly revealed she had been undergoing treatment after she saw a post online from someone who had seen her at the hospital. She was obviously terrified someone would leak the news before she could share it herself. That's the thing with fame, it's not right, but you do have to sacrifice your privacy in that respect. You have no control. And like Sarah, Tom didn't want to be outed.

It was important to Tom to get across the facts. But most importantly, he wanted to share his story in his own words. He wanted to give other people strength and help those who might be going through something similar. It was typical Tom to take the bull by the horns and lead from the front. It's his Leo traits coming out again.

We decided we wanted to share the news with OK! so

With And Without You

Tom's manager called and spoke to their celebrity journalist, Kirsty Hatcher.

Kirsty had covered our wedding years earlier and had interviewed us many times over the years, so we thought it was only right to share this latest life event with the magazine that had supported us. Plus, we trusted Kirsty with our story and we knew she would handle it super sensitively. We didn't want this sensationalised and Tom's manager Damien was keen the magazine didn't use the phrase 'terminal cancer'. Yes, it was terminal, but the phrase is so negative and immediately makes you think of death and we wanted to keep our story as positive as possible – Tom has an inoperable tumour and he was going to fight it with every fibre of his body.

The magazine editors agreed and were amazing on the day of the shoot. By this point the chemo and radiotherapy was making Tom feel very weak and sick, but he got through it like a trouper. The biggest struggle was actually the interview. Tom found it really hard to talk – the chemo made his speech slur a bit – but even if he could speak properly, I don't think he would have been able to get the words out. It was the first time he had actually spoken about his diagnosis in such detail and I could tell it was hard for him. I felt like I needed to fill in the gaps and did most of

Dark Days Of Summer

the talking, as usual! For once, I think Tom was secretly pleased that I took control in that instance.

Of course our close friends and family already knew about Tom's diagnosis. I had called Tom's mum Noreen once we had the glioblastoma diagnosis. I remember feeling so angry about it that I was actually quite brutal.

'Yep, it's the worst case scenario,' I told her. 'It's not what they thought, it's worse. If you Google it, it will probably say the prognosis is really bad but we didn't get that far, so yes, pretty much the worst case scenario.'

'OK,' she replied. Obviously she was devastated, but I had to be honest. I had the worst job of calling everyone to tell them that Tom had the worst tumour you could probably get. Looking back, would I change the way I told people? I don't think I would. I had to be honest, I had to lay down the facts and I had to tell people we were going to get through it. Also, Noreen has known me for 13 years by this point, so she knows I'm not going to sugarcoat anything for her and she appreciated that.

I remember them coming down to see us after that, the first time they had seen him since his diagnosis, and his dad Nige just broke down. Then Tom started breaking down. They were both crying.

With And Without You

'Right you two,' I remember saying. 'No more of that. We are going to beat this.' I know it sounds so harsh, but I just knew that crying wasn't getting us anywhere. I knew Tom like the back of my hand. Sitting there crying would just bring him down and he needed to be strong. We all did. As horrible as it sounds, I felt like saying to people you can cry, but not around Tom. Cry in private. He needs to be told he will beat this.

Once Tom's family knew, it was then time to tell the boys. He told Jay first and then I called Max. Jay called Siva to tell him while Max called Nathan. Somehow it was easier for them to tell the boys. It saved Tom repeating himself and I could tell it was exhausting him. I also imagine it's hard to take on other people's emotions and reactions when you are going through it yourself. It certainly didn't get any easier the more people we told.

Obviously the boys were as shocked and gutted as we were, but they were so supportive and rallied around Tom immediately. Jay came over straight away and started researching the type of tumour Tom had – I think that in hindsight it was his way of processing it all.

Out of all of them, Max took it quite badly. Max and Tom were very close and would always share a room together when they were on tour. They were like brothers. Every time Max called and spoke to Tom he was in bits, then it would set Tom off and they would be in bits together. It was just so sad. At the time, Max was on Strictly and I think that training and the rehearsals gave him a distraction from it all. I know watching him gave Tom a bit of a distraction, and even though it was too risky for Tom to go and watch him live from the studio, it didn't stop him from taking the piss out of his dance moves and sequins from home.

Meanwhile, like Jay, I threw myself into a rabbit hole of information and started looking at all kinds of different treatments. I felt like I needed to do something to help. I was determined to find the cure the doctors were saying didn't exist. If I just sat there and cried every day then I would be no help to anyone and most importantly I would be no help to Tom – he would just absorb that negativity. I had to hold it together. I also had to be strong for Aurelia, and the baby I was carrying.

If someone had told me my life was going to be researching tumours and taking Tom to radiotherapy in London every day at 36 weeks pregnant, I wouldn't have believed them.

I spent hours on the phone to doctors all over the world,

emailing people, reading up on alternative therapies. I knew everything there was to know about glioblastomas.

It was a weird role reversal for me and Tom, as he had been the one to take care of everything before – like I said, he would sort out the bills, mortgage, etc. If we needed a quote for some building work or repair then Tom would take care of it. But now I was in the driving seat, I was the one finding out everything we needed to know to try and help us navigate this situation.

It became like a full time job. I wasn't looking after myself and wasn't sleeping. I feel terrible saying it now, but there were moments when I forgot I was even pregnant.

Everything was about Tom and keeping him well and healthy, and of course positive.

Aurelia was too young to understand Daddy's diagnosis, but she knew something was going on. She never saw us cry, we always made sure we were never sad in front of her, but she must have picked up something from our moods or subconscious. Kids are amazing like that. Suddenly, she became a bit of a minx and was really unsettled. It was even more reason for us to keep things as positive and normal as possible.

I started looking at clinical trials abroad, meanwhile Tom

began physiotherapy to help with his mobility. The tumour and the treatment could sometimes make him unsteady on his feet and he found it helped. He also had reiki and did yoga sessions to help with his strength. Tom was open to anything and everything and threw himself into it all. I think the more relaxing treatments, like reiki and yoga, allowed him to switch off for a bit, and give him a short moment of peace where he didn't have to think about the tumour or chemo.

I think I probably processed the diagnosis better than Tom, but of course I did because it wasn't me going through it. Although we did always say if it was the other way around that Tom would be useless and wouldn't know what to do or how to cope.

As the days passed, I could see it was all starting to consume him.

The weight of his diagnosis was resting heavy on his shoulders and he was feeling weak from treatment. But despite everything he was going through, he still had this super power and wanted to survive.

'Are you hoping for a miracle?' Kirsty asked.

'I need everyone's love and positivity. I'm going to fight this,' Tom said.

With And Without You

'Have you got your head around the idea that you may not be around for your children's future?' Kirsty asked.

'No,' Tom said. 'Because I am going to be here, I am going to fight this.'

Tom's message was clear, he was not going to give in.

SEPTEMBER 2022
30th One year since the SU2C concert

7

Song Of Hope

'My grief never leaves me, so to have people there for me every day is something I am forever grateful for'

Tom decided quite early on that he wanted to do as much as he possibly could to raise awareness for brain tumours. He found it shocking that there was hardly any funding and that so little was known by the wider public about glioblastomas.

He made it his mission to use his platform to get the message out there – but to also share his story. He wanted to help inspire others going through the same thing and for them to have and share the same positivity and beliefs that he did. He wanted other people to have hope.

'I think that I should write a book,' he told me one day. 'I think it would be good for me to get everything down on paper, it might help other people.'

Tom never failed to amaze me during his illness. He just always found the time and energy to help other people. But it was typical Tom. He wasn't ever one to sit down for five minutes. He was always on the go, buzzing around.

Song Of Hope

And he certainly wasn't going to sit around and do nothing during his treatment, even at his lowest, darkest moments, his mind would still be running at 100 miles an hour. It's inspiring really, and I was so proud of him for wanting to do something to help other people.

I thought the book was an amazing idea and it didn't take him long to come up with his book title, 'Hope'. Tom was determined to write it himself. He worked with a ghost writer, Grant Brydon, who would help him form the chapters and structure of the book, but Tom spent many nights on the sofa on his laptop just writing his story. Writing from the heart.

As soon as he got a publisher on board, Blink Publishing, Tom announced the news on his Instagram:

'Hi, I'm Tom Parker, a lot of you know me as one fifth of The Wanted, but I am also a father, a husband, and a son that's battling brain cancer. My book, coming this July, is not about dying: it's a book about living. It's a book about finding hope in whatever situation you're dealt, and living your best life no matter what. It will show you how having faith in hope and daring to dream means you can carry on, against all odds.'

With And Without You

Tom's Instagram went wild with lots of fans promising to buy his book. He also opened himself up to a whole new fan base, to others who are battling cancer and saw Tom as an inspirational figure who gave them hope.

In September 2021, just over a year after his diagnosis, Tom started to document everything for his book. We were also approached by a production company, Spun Gold, about doing a documentary. Tom worked with their producer Nick Bullen on *The Full Monty* and he couldn't think of anyone better to team up with to help him share his story.

As well as the book, Tom also wanted to put on a concert. After all, music was his big love and Stand Up To Cancer was the right fit. The documentary would mean the cameras would be filming us in the weeks leading up to the concert which took place at the Royal Albert Hall on September 20th.

While Tom felt that writing the book was therapeutic, he thought the documentary would give people a real view of what living with cancer was like. He knew that his platform as a pop star would get people talking about tumours and ask the question why so little goes into brain cancer research when it is responsible for killing so many children and those under 40 every year.

Song Of Hope

We let the cameras into our home and they filmed 24/7. I told them from the beginning that they were not going to come into our house and get the tears. That was not what our house was about. We woke up happy, we started our days with a smile and we were not going to be sad. You will see there are videos of us dancing, mucking around, being with the kids. Tom and I believed what you put in is what you get back, so we had no time to be sitting around moping. We were going to carry on as normal.

The crew filmed everything, from Tom getting up in the night to when he had just had treatments and was recovering from the effects of that. Tom wanted the documentary to be a real reflection of what life was like for him, I suppose to normalise it too. He wanted to show people that you can live with cancer. It isn't a death sentence. He wanted to show people that cancer can affect anyone and none of us know what's around the corner or what life has planned for us. He wanted to be honest about the alternative treatments and therapies he was using, to show that there is more on offer than what's currently available on the NHS, that everyone's cancer journey is different and you should do what is right for you.

Treatment for this type of brain cancer hasn't changed

in 30 years. When you think of the developments in breast cancer and the vaccine available now for teenage girls to prevent the HPV (the virus which most commonly causes cervical cancer), it feels like the rest of the cancer world is moving but the brain cancer world is stuck in the 1990s. You are given the option of chemo and radio and are then told that if that goes well you will get another round of chemo, and we will see then where we are at.

'That's it?' I asked the doctor. 'Anything else?'

'No, that's it,' he said.

We found out from our own research, Tom and I, that there was other stuff out there that could help people with brain tumours, things the NHS could invest in, but they don't get sufficient funding from the government.

Tom wanted to be up front about the fact he was exploring beyond what the NHS could offer. His NHS team was amazing, but even their hands were tied. If they had the budget to bring in the treatments that are used in Spain or America, they would bring it to the UK in a heartbeat. But it all comes down to money essentially. Is it because the prognosis is so poor that they just don't bother? Surely the goal is to improve the prognosis. That was Tom's end goal and the documentary fed into that.

Song Of Hope

I doubt it was easy for Tom to film all of the time. The camera team and production staff from Spun Gold were amazing, but there were times after Tom was diagnosed when he felt exposed and vulnerable as someone living with cancer, so it wasn't always easy for him.

When he was in his family bubble with me, Rae and Bodhi, we kept his spirits up. When my family was over or we were at my mum's for dinner, there was no feeling down. When we saw his parents, we had no time for tears. But I suppose, outside of the family unit, which was basically his security blanket, he felt a bit of pressure to be the mouthpiece for brain cancer, which was fine, but he didn't want it all to be doom and gloom. He didn't want to pay the cancer attention. He always said it wasn't like he was ignoring it, but if he paid it attention it would mean a bad day for him. He didn't want the title or label of a cancer sufferer or victim, but someone who is living with cancer, so it was important to him that the documentary wasn't sad, but positive and inspirational.

Tom also needed to think about who he wanted to perform at the concert. His first thought was his old band mates. By this point, the band had been split up for seven years and Tom was slightly apprehensive about it. They won't mind me saying as they have said it all themselves, but they did have a few fall-outs between them over the years, and there was some friction towards the end, so Tom was worried that no one would want to do it.

He sent them all a message each to ask the question and then they set up a Zoom. He was quite nervous to see them all, especially as he had been undergoing treatment and looked quite different – he had lost weight, for example. He lost about three and half stone in three weeks when he first started having treatment and the chemo made him feel so rotten and have such a loss of appetite that he really struggled to put it back on. But I don't know why Tom was so worried. As soon as they all got on the call it was like they were, back in the day.

I guess when you are in a close group of friends and you have that bond and the strong foundations of a friendship, time can pass, but you know you will always have each other. That's how Tom saw the boys, his brothers, and he was absolutely over the moon when they all agreed to do it.

Afterwards Tom set up a call with his manager Damien, who was a really good friend to Tom, and they pulled together their dream list of people to perform at the concert.

I know Tom was really keen to have Ed Sheeran there.

Song Of Hope

Ed had heard about Tom's diagnosis and offered to pay for the treatment which was an amazing thing to do. After everything he had done for him, Tom definitely wanted him as part of the line-up.

Tom was also good friends with McFly's Harry Judd and went to school with Danny, so he put in a call to see if Harry and the boys would be up for performing – and they were. Tom was so made up. KSI, Becky Hill and Sigrid also agreed to perform. Capital radio DJs Roman Kemp and Sonny Jay agreed to host.

Then, Tom got a message out of the blue from Liam Payne of One Direction. He wasn't someone he was expecting to hear from, especially given that The Wanted and One Direction had a huge falling out about 10 years earlier.

Both bands had been at the height of their fame back in 2012, and it seemed the fans and press thought there wasn't enough room for both of them. There were quite a few little digs that started off, I suppose, as boy band banter, but ended up turning into a bitter fall-out on Twitter.

I think it all started when Louis Tomlinson was papped reading The Wanted book in a pound shop – he found it hilarious that their book was so cheap and I suppose the inference was that the boys were cheap too.

With And Without You

Then a few months later, The Wanted were on Chris Moyles' BBC Radio 1 show to promote *I Found You* and Chris, obviously aware of the rivalry, appeared to wind them up by saying that One Direction were more popular than they were.

Tom jumped in and replied, 'Our new single *I Found You* is a bit different. We like to mix it up. We try not to be stereotypical.'

It was seen as a bit of a dig by One Direction fans that Tom was saying all of One Direction's songs sounded the same. And it seemed the band thought so too. Harry Styles took to Twitter and wrote, 'Chris Moyles is actually right though… If 1D weren't in the picture, The Wanted would've been WAY more popular!'

They also didn't like that Max had said their new single was better than One Direction's new music with Nathan then telling Chris, 'Ha, much better.'

Louis quoted Max and Nathan on Twitter and wrote 'not sure' only for Nathan to hit back 'truth hurts'.

It was all a bit ridiculous really and something out of a school playground, but the fans were taking it seriously. You were either Team One Direction or Team The Wanted and it was impossible to be in between and like both!

Song Of Hope

A few months later, it all got a bit personal where they were throwing insults at each other over Twitter. Zayn called Max 'a geek', Tom told Zayn he was getting his knickers in a twist, Louis insulted Tom's appearance, then Zayn took it a step too far when he called Max 'chlamydia boy'.

Max then said, 'Tell me your problems without the security in NYC. The only problem I have with you is the shit banter. Grow up son.' And then Zayn replied calling Max 'a clown'. As I say, it was all quite childish really, but the feud was very real.

So when Tom got a message from Liam, you can see why he was a bit taken aback. Liam said he was inspired by Tom and had to reach out to him after reading about his story and Tom asked him if he wanted to perform at the gig.

They arranged a Zoom call to talk it all through. I think Tom was a bit nervous as they hadn't ever spoken before and he didn't want it to feel awkward and weird, but in the end, him and Liam got on so well.

I know how much it meant to Tom to have Liam reach out to him and for him to come and perform that day. After that, they became mates and Liam was actually with us at Tom's funeral. I still keep in touch with him now. He will check in on me every now and then to see if me and the kids are OK. He doesn't have to do it, but he does and it means a lot. There are some people I don't hear from who I thought might have stayed in contact, so it's lovely that Liam remembers us, especially given Liam and Tom were not always so close.

One thing I've learned on my grief journey, is to be grateful for the people who are there for us all the time. I couldn't have done any of this without my mum or my auntie Ju. They do everything for me and the kids. If I am working in London, Julie will pick the kids up, take them home, feed them and cook me a dinner too. My mum will sit and play with them while I am writing this book, or doing a podcast. You take for granted having a partner who is your teammate, who you share the duties with, and when they are gone, a big hole is left.

My 'little village' as I call them are not just there for the anniversaries, Christmases and birthdays. They say once the funeral is over that people slip away and get on with their own lives, but I'm lucky that I've not been left alone. They know that I think about Tom every single day, and I need support every day, not just when those important milestones come around.

My grief never leaves me, so to have people there for

Song Of Hope

me every day, or even just now and then, is something I am forever grateful for.

As the date of the gig got closer, I remember Tom started to worry a bit. It wasn't unusual for him to worry, but he seemed quite anxious. Firstly, the boys had never played at the Royal Albert Hall, so for Tom it was such a big deal. It's an iconic venue for music stars, so it meant the world to Tom to perform there. It certainly cranked up the nerves. He didn't want anything to go wrong.

Of course, alongside the usual preparation for such a big concert, there was still the issue of Tom's health. Chemo had made his voice change and it wasn't as strong as it used to be. Tom was also starting to have mobility issues, and he was worried he wouldn't be able to physically perform. Being on stage and singing was everything to Tom. It made him feel at home. In a weird way, performing to thousands gave him security.

Tom hired a vocal coach, Steven Luke Walker, to help him get his voice ready for the gig. Steven would come to our house and spend hours with Tom. It was important for Tom to get his voice back to what it was, but also not to push it so far that it would crack altogether and he would lose it. That would have been devastating for Tom. He also had physio to improve the mobility in his arm and leg where he had lost the movement. Tom was used to jumping around the stage like a lunatic so he hated the fact that he couldn't move in the way he wanted.

In fact, as we got closer to the night of the concert, I think Tom was more worried about his mobility than his voice. I really think that deep down he was conscious that people would notice and would immediately think he was gravely ill. It was important to Tom to keep that mental resilience. If fans started noticing his lack of movement then it would get into his head and the negative thoughts would return. So Tom worked really hard to get his strength up for the big night and the production team made sure he was comfortable on set, having places where he felt supported if he needed it.

In the end Tom had nothing to worry about. Typical Tom panicking about stuff going wrong and then it never does. The concert went according to plan and The Wanted were incredible! It was such a great night and raised so much money, £31,169,340 for Stand Up To Cancer and The National Brain Appeal, an important charity which raises money for The National Hospital for Neurology &

Song Of Hope

Neurosurgery, where Tom had lots of scans and his treatment. The concert was so successful that The Wanted announced a greatest hits album and a 2022 tour.

Tom was so excited about that. He had brought the boys back together, thinking it would be for one night, only for them all to agree to go back on tour. If Tom could have had one wish, apart from good health, it would have been to get back on stage with the boys and do what he loved and did best.

It gave Tom just the boost he needed. Something for him to focus on and look forward to. It gave him hope. And there was more good news to come.

A few weeks later, Tom went for a routine scan at the hospital and was told by his consultant that the tumour had shrunk and was showing as stable. Tom was so happy, he burst into tears. He couldn't wait to share the news with everyone who had supported him.

Opening up his Instagram page, he started tapping into his phone…

'I'm sitting here with tears in my eyes. We've got my brain tumour under control. We had the results from my latest scan… and I'm delighted to say it is STABLE. Such a mix of emotions. We couldn't ask for any more really at this point; a year or so into this journey. Honestly, over the moon. We can sleep a little easier tonight. Thank you for all your love and support over the last 12+ months.'

'At last', I remember thinking 'a bit of good news.'

But now as I sit here, in September 2022, I can't believe how much has changed in a year. This time last year we both had so much hope, now I'm sat here without my husband.

I would say these last six months without Tom have been a rollercoaster of emotions.

I feel angry when I look back and remember a year ago that his tumour was stable – why did he deteriorate? Why did he have to leave us? I've also felt the biggest hole in my heart and it physically hurts. It's like I have a weight sitting on my chest. Grief can feel so heavy, but I know I will feel lighter again. One day.

OCTOBER 2022

20th Bodhi's second birthday

8

A Guiding Light

'Bodhi arrived at a time when we needed light in our lives – he gave Tom a sense of purpose'

It's October 2022 and Bodhi is turning two. I find myself looking at him and I still feel nothing but guilt. Two years on and I still feel guilty that he didn't get to experience the Daddy Tom that Rae did.

I guess my mum could say that about me, and although they are very different circumstances, I didn't have the bond with my dad that my brothers had with theirs. I have to tell myself it's a fact of life and I can't do anything about it. And despite my own guilt and sadness over Bodhi's first months, it doesn't seem to have affected him. He is the cheekiest, happiest little boy and he is the image of Tom. He is a typical little two-year-old into his toys, cars and Spiderman and he idolises his big sister. He's a good sleeper, he's calm and he eats everything that's put in front of him, be it spaghetti bolognese or beans on toast. He just loves his food.

We had the name Bodhi chosen before even Aurelia was born – it was top of the list of our boys' names. Little did we

A Guiding Light

know at the time that we'd be expecting a son when Tom was given the news he had an inoperable brain tumour and that the name would mean so much more.

I remember we were watching *Point Break* with my little brother Bobbie when I was expecting Aurelia and he turned to me and said, 'Kels, I love the name Bodhi.' Tom and I looked at each other and we were like, 'We're not sure.'

But the more we thought about it, the more it grew on us, though probably me more than Tom in the end. When we found out we were expecting a son, we knew he had to be a Bodhi. Tom still wasn't 100 per cent set on it. He wanted to call him Paris, don't ask me why, he just liked the name, and probably thought it was 'out there' and cool, but I didn't – I am from south east London, I couldn't call my son Paris! In the end I told him, 'We are having Bodhi and that's the end of it!'

Being of Sanskrit origin, the name means 'awakening' and 'enlightenment'. It is connected to the concept of nirvana and the final goal of Buddhism. By finally being free of greed and ego, those who achieve nirvana reach a state of bliss and peace. It was so apt for our situation at the time of his birth, with Tom being diagnosed weeks earlier. We saw our son as a gift and the light at the end of our tunnel. It's mad that we had that name picked out long, long before Tom got ill. Years before in fact. Like Aurelia, the kids' names have such important meanings when I look back now. 'The golden one' and 'enlightenment' – there are no coincidences, they were meant to be.

I found out I was pregnant with Bodhi nine months after Aurelia was born. There was definitely nothing wrong with Tom's sperm count, ha ha. I wouldn't say we were actively trying, but I wasn't on contraception either so I can't say it was a total surprise. We wanted another child but we didn't think it would happen that quickly. In retrospect, Bodhi was conceived at the right time in terms of what happened months later.

I think I was around seven weeks pregnant when we were invited to a birthday party. Tom got so drunk that he went around telling everyone we were having a baby. I could have killed him. Tom loved being a dad, it was the best job in the world to him, and I think he was just excited. Just maybe a bit too much!

My pregnancy with Bodhi was pretty textbook. I was worried about preeclampsia again – though it is ridiculous saying that was my worry now knowing what our situation was to be when Bodhi arrived.

A Guiding Light

We decided to find out the sex this time. I wanted to get organised. Aurelia was still young and I had a lot of her baby bits still in her wardrobe. We thought it would be a practical thing to do to find out. If it was another girl, they could wear all of the beautiful pink outfits I had for her, and if it was a boy I could give them away and start from scratch.

When we found out we were expecting a boy, we were over the moon. I remember my friend Jemma saying, 'Oh my God, you're literally like the 2.4 family now, aren't you? How perfect can you be?'

I thought about it myself. One of each – it couldn't be more perfect.

Again, looking back I believe there was another, more spiritual reason for us finding out it was a boy. I think that knowing the sex of the baby this time around gave Tom more strength and fight.

Bodhi was born on October 20th, 2020, weighing 6lb 3oz at the same hospital where I gave birth to Aurelia 16 months earlier.

I remember we were watching TOWIE and at around 10pm my waters broke. I had no contractions so I called my mum to tell her he was coming. 'Get some sleep, then ring me,' she said.

But I didn't get much sleep at all. I spent much of the night awake waiting for the contractions to come and still nothing. At 7am, I called my mum again to tell her there was still no movement and then I called the midwife. I had my heart set on a home birth, so the midwife came to check me over.

'I think that you might need to be induced,' she told me. 'I know that's not what you want, but we need to get things started there.' I really didn't want to be induced again but that said, I wasn't prepared to take any risks, so I went to hospital, albeit reluctantly. I had wanted a home birth with Bodhi. I didn't want another labour like Aurelia's, I wanted this one to be more peaceful with less intervention. I wanted to actually do the hypnobirthing I had started when pregnant with Aurelia. But the most important reason for a home birth was Tom. I didn't want Tom picking up infections at the hospital, especially if we were going to be there for ages like we were with Aurelia. He would also be more comfortable at home. We felt like it was a safer bet all round if we opted for a home birth. But obviously it wasn't meant to be.

At the hospital, the midwife had tried pessaries to start my labour but nothing was happening. 'This baby has

A Guiding Light

broken its own waters but doesn't want to show up,' I joked to Tom and the nurses.

I was trying to keep Tom's spirits up. He had been taking chemo tablets and they had left him exhausted and very sick. He was thin and pale and had already lost his hair.

'I am meant to be the one throwing up, not you,' I would tell him, but inside all I could feel was guilt. It was almost like an out-of-body experience. I felt awful that I couldn't look after Tom while I was in labour. I had been doing everything for him from the moment he was diagnosed until we got to the maternity ward, and I felt so bad that I was giving birth and not being there for him. I know it's silly. I was giving birth to our baby. But that is how I felt.

An hour passed by at the hospital and still nothing. The midwives decided to put me on a hormone drip, then within two minutes I could feel something happening.

'It worked!' I said to Tom.

'At bloody last!' he said to me, his eyes wide with excitement. It was the first time he perked up the whole time we were there.

Thirty minutes later and Bodhi was in my arms. Our beautiful baby boy. Our little saviour. Our son who will carry on the Parker name. I looked at Tom and he was crying his eyes out, and then that set me off. The emotion of it all became too much and he took himself off to the bathroom. 'Is he OK?' the midwife asked.

'Yes, he's fine. He's just got a brain tumour,' I told her. She looked at me stunned. She wasn't expecting me to say that. 'He's having treatment' I continued. 'He's only just been diagnosed.'

I think it all just completely overwhelmed Tom. He was over the moon that our baby was here, our first son, and he was crying tears of joy, but I also think there was an element of fear for him. He was probably thinking, 'Will I beat this? How long have I got left with this baby?' It's heartbreaking to think what might have been going through his mind.

Then the guilt hit me again – what world have we brought our beautiful baby boy into? What are his first months going to be like as I ferry Tom to and from appointments? 'There won't be any time for a baby bubble,' I thought.

'Snap out of it, Kelsey!' I quickly and quietly told myself. This boy is a blessing, he has the most amazing daddy and big sister, and Tom is going to be around at home, while most dads have to go back to work. It was the perspective I needed.

Taking Bodhi home to meet Aurelia was magical. She

A Guiding Light

was so in awe of her baby brother. Before he was born we had bought her a dolly. I read it was a nice way to introduce a new baby to a little one, to get them used to the baby and they get to look after it. And now baby Bodhi was home, and Rae was so happy to have a 'real' dolly. She doted on him so much, it was adorable.

'She is going to be one amazing big sister,' Tom said to me. And he was right. I think there is a reason Aurelia came first. She is strong and independent and I know when she is older she will be able to hold her own. She is protective too, and even though they sometimes argue like cat and dog, I know she will always have her little brother's back. Rae has all the qualities of the perfect older sibling. Bodhi is a lot more calm and chilled and it balances her out.

As Rae planted a kiss on her new baby brother's head, for a single split second I forgot about Tom's cancer, something that had been the centre of our world for months. In that moment, as Rae stroked her brother's head, everything was so perfect. Our little family of four. Life couldn't be more perfect.

Bodhi's first birthday without Tom was a tough one. Bodhi arrived at a time when we needed light in our lives, and now it felt like we were in darkness again without Tom. We threw him a massive party, Spiderman-themed of course, and he loved it, even though I'm aware he will have no memory of this when he is older. It was a bittersweet day because on his first birthday, Bodhi had taken his first steps, and Tom was there to see it now. A year later and he is running around, talking, dancing, and is fully in that toddler stage of his life. Tom's missed all that.

I remember the day before he turned two, I was thinking about the day he arrived, the sadness Tom felt. And now I am sitting here feeling sad about all the things the children will miss out on by not having their dad here. Would Tom be enrolling Bodhi into Little Kickers now? Would he have bought him his first Bolton football shirt as a birthday present?

Bodhi has started to speak now, and one of the words Tom won't ever hear is 'Dada'. It's not fair.

When Bodhi was born it really gave Tom a sense of purpose. He was a distraction for Tom and all what was going on. Around that time, Tom was going through intense rounds of chemotherapy and radiotherapy that made him feel dreadful. Tom always said he wouldn't wish chemotherapy on his worst enemy, it was so brutal. He was scared of the impact of chemotherapy, both mentally and physically, as his nan had been through it years before after she was diagnosed with lung cancer. Tom had a lasting memory of his nan and how ill and frail she had become by a medicine that was there to make her better.

And that's how Tom felt when he started his treatment too. He was so sick, extremely fatigued and weak. He didn't want to eat as everything tasted like metal and his mouth was covered in ulcers. People always say that chemotherapy doesn't just kill off all the bad cells in your body, but the good ones too. And Tom definitely felt like everything had been zapped out of him.

Tom had to take his chemotherapy tablets a short while before he had his radio – the doctors said that this way they could both work together as a two-pronged attack on the tumour.

The chemotherapy works by killing cancer cells that are about to split into two, and therefore stopping them dividing again into four, then eight, and so on and causing a growth or spread. Radiotherapy on the other hand will use radiation to specifically target the tumour. It will pump all the radiation directly into the tumour, trying to avoid as many healthy cells close to it as possible. But that didn't come without its side effects either and Tom felt like he had been knocked out after it. It made him so tired and weak. He couldn't ever go up to King's College Hospital on his own, not that I would let him anyway, but he would be far too weak to have come back alone.

The only things that got him through those dark moments of treatment were the children. He loved getting up with them in the morning when he could, and while he might be too weak or tired to do their breakfast or play with them, he loved nothing more than giving them a cuddle on the sofa, watching TV together.

It pains me to say that I feel like Bodhi missed out a lot on the 'real' Tom. He didn't have the daddy that Aurelia had. The bouncing around, lively dad that Tom was. I do wonder if deep down Tom's soul knew he wouldn't be here and that's why Bodhi didn't get the attention Rae did. I mean, don't get me wrong, Tom was a bloody amazing dad to Bodhi, he loved him so, so much. But when I had Rae, Tom wanted to know where I was taking her, what time I was feeding her, all of those things. And Bodhi just didn't get that. Was it that Tom couldn't, I don't know, go there with him? Because of his soul. Did he know he would soon be leaving him?

A Guiding Light

Rae and Bodhi meant everything to Tom. As a pop star in a huge band, he achieved so much, won awards, sold millions of records and travelled the world on tours, but the thing that gave him his purpose and what he was most proud of were his kids.

He helped to teach them so much – how to roll, how to sit up, how to walk – but they taught him so much too. Rae taught him that you can do and achieve anything – her spirit and drive always impressed him, even at her young age. 'She will be on stage one day,' he would always say. Bodhi taught him calmness and patience. Tom was a big ball of energy and always on the go. Even when he was sitting down, he was moving, mind racing with ideas. Bodhi is such a chilled little boy, so laid back, and I think that his relaxed nature and sense of easiness brought Tom some tranquillity and peace. It's OK to slow down and enjoy the moment.

Tom had always said that having Rae and Bodhi made him grow up so quickly. As I've said, Tom was a bit of a party animal and 4am would be an early night for him back in the day. But as soon as he became a dad, he became this wonderful nurturing person and it made me love him more, if that was even possible. To him, his little family were everything, and to us he was the world.

NOVEMBER 2022

22nd My 100km charity trek in the Sahara

9

Stepping Out

'When a butterfly flew past me as I got to the top of a sand dune, I very much knew it was Tom. I bet he was saying something like, 'Hi babe, you are mad doing this!''

Giovanna Fletcher has become a good friend over the years. We have a lot in common, both mums to little ones and both married to singers in a boyband. A few months after Tom died, she invited me on her podcast, 'Happy Mum, Happy Baby'. I had done a few bits and pieces after Tom died, I had been on Loose Women and Lorraine and had done a couple of interviews with the press, all to raise awareness for brain tumours and tell Tom's story.

During the podcast I spoke about my guilt of having a baby while Tom was so ill. It was the first time I had really told anyone else how I felt and I found it quite emotional. There were quite a few tears. Recalling the moment Tom cuddled Bodhi, I broke down to Gi. 'Oh, it was just awful... Tom was so emotional, but obviously Tom was emotional for a different reason this time – he was thinking how long will I have left with this baby. Oh God, that's quite sad.'

Stepping Out

Gi is such a calming and soothing person, which is probably why I felt I could open up to her. She replied, 'In many ways Bodhi is probably going to grow up just thankful that his dad was there.'

'Oh yeah, he'll just be happy that his dad witnessed his birth,' I told her, 'but I just felt sorry for Tom. Because Tom was in this place where he just wasn't Tom anymore – the moment he got diagnosed, I lost Tom.'

It was something I had felt for the last 18 months of Tom's life, but not something I had said in public. I didn't grieve Tom in his final months as I didn't believe he was going to die, but grieved the person he was. I had lost my funny, jokey, sometimes annoying husband! Looking back now I think his soul was just slowly fading, his sparkle was going, and then eventually his light went out.

After the podcast I chatted to Giovanna and she told me about a charity trek she was doing in November to raise money for CoppaFeel, a breast cancer charity she is a patron of. She was looking for captains to lead teams on a 100 kilometre walk through the Sahara Desert.

If there is anything I had learned from Tom it was to seize every opportunity with both hands, and I knew this would be something very worthwhile. On the trek I would be meeting cancer survivors, those still living with cancer, and those like me who had lost loved ones to cancer, all while raising money for an amazing cause. I felt I could not only learn from them, but hopefully share my own grief journey and knowledge too.

I definitely found my spiritual side during Tom's illness. I felt like I had finally woken up. I started to see things differently in life and I started to see life differently. I guess in the same way Tom always had. I had always been a very positive person, but I realised how important the mind was in healing, and that was one of the reasons why I didn't want Tom looking at stuff on the internet, falling down a rabbit hole of negativity. It made me look more into alternative therapies and what else is out there to get rid of the tumours.

When Tom was first diagnosed he was offered the standard radiotherapy and chemotherapy, but even before he started the treatment I knew it wouldn't be enough. Brain cancer charities only get one per cent of government funding, which means the treatment options are limited. I couldn't just accept what was being offered – I knew there would be more treatments out there that are not available on the NHS, or alternative therapies that could help.

In my research, I came across Dave Bolton, one of the

Baby number two I found out I was pregnant with Bodhi nine months after Aurelia was born. We wanted another child but we didn't think it would happen that quickly!

Bodhi Parker Bodhi was born on October 20, 2020, weighing 6lb 3oz at the same hospital where I gave birth to Aurelia 16 months earlier

Turning one On his first birthday, Bodhi had taken his first steps and I was so glad Tom was there to see it. It's hard to believe a year later he's a walking, talking toddler

Last Christmas On Tom's last Christmas he was feeling happy and healthy. We just moved into our new family home and for the first time in a long time we felt there was some normality in our lives again

You are my world
Never in a million years did I ever think that I would be a widow at 31. I mean, who does? It's the club no one wants to ever join. I have learned in the past 18 months that your grief will never, ever go away, you just have to learn to live around it. I am never going to forget Tom but I now have to live my life without him

Never forget you
I remember making the decision early on that the children wouldn't be going to the funeral. They were far too young. Instead, they made a picture for Tom with their handprints and I placed it on top of his coffin

Remembering you It was a special moment when my late grandad said he wanted Tom to join our family on the memory bench. It shows how important Tom was to my family

Young man I have no doubt that Bodhi will grow into an amazing man just like Tom, albeit in a much calmer fashion

Budding star Aurelia already has the makings of a total star. She's a natural born performer, very much like her dad

Trick or Treat
For Halloween the kids dressed up as characters from their favourite movie *Sing*. Bodhi looks so cute in his Buster Moon suit

First Christmas
The first Christmas without Tom was tough. The hardest part was writing gift tags just from me. 'To Rae, to Bo, Merry Christmas, Lots of love Mummy'. It just didn't look right

Tom's game We organised a charity football match in Tom's honour at our local football club, Bromley FC, where almost 3,000 people came out to watch a bunch of celebrities play. We raised over £25,000 for brain tumour charities

CoppaFeel trek Here's a photo of myself and my team after the Coppafeel trek through the Sahara. We walked over 100km to raise awareness and funds for breast cancer research

Milestones
Aurelia graduated from preschool this year and will be starting big school this September. It feels like only a few months ago she was in my arms at the hospital

Ahead of the Game Dave Bolton was like a beacon of wisdom. He knew everything there was to know about glioblastomas and helped Tom and I through our toughest challenges

Looking ahead What does the future hold? In truth, I don't know. I am going to live for today, be present for my children and be the best mummy I possibly can

Stepping Out

very few people in the world who has survived 10 years with a grade four glioblastoma. In 2014, he was diagnosed with a cancerous tumour on the front lobe of his brain. They operated on him and he was given a prognosis of five years. But when he went back the following year for a routine brain scan, they discovered a glioblastoma and told him he had six to eight months to live. Just three if he didn't have the treatment.

Ten years earlier, Dave had been involved in a horrific bike crash that almost killed him. A huge lorry practically crushed him on his motorbike and he was in a coma for eight days. He had an operation and was warned he may lose his leg, but the doctors managed to save it. Dave was told that although his leg was saved, he wouldn't ever walk again. But Dave was so determined and worked so hard on his rehabilitation that just 18 months after the accident, he was back in his day job as a police officer and competing in all the sports he loved, like rugby and kickboxing.

Dave was going to tackle the glioblastoma in the same way he did his bike crash – with positivity and determination. He was ready for the fight. However, just as his chemo and radiotherapy was coming to an end, he had a breakdown. He was admitted to a psychiatric hospital where he spent weeks recovering. At that point, Dave knew he needed something else to try and tackle the tumour and used his own research and things he learned from his own diagnosis to set up Ahead of the Game Foundation.

The charity is amazing and offers so many alternative therapies that are not available through the NHS, but help people like Tom and Dave. In his clinic he has oxygen therapy, red light therapy and even a personal trainer who helps patients with their diets and fitness. I had read so many stories of people using oxygen and red light therapy and getting stable scans. Obviously, we all need oxygen, but when you have an illness like cancer it's important to get as much oxygen in you as possible as it gets our stem cells to start healing us. An oxygen machine does this and gets it into your system quickly. It's also said to fight any infections or bacteria in your body, and that's why it's so important to get fresh air. Red light therapy targets cancer cells but causes them to swell and then basically explode and die. It was something Tom wanted to try, so I messaged Dave.

Tom began visiting Dave and using his treatments. Dave is like a beacon of wisdom. He knows everything there is to know about a glioblastoma and what helps to keep it stable, and what doesn't. And who better to take advice

Stepping Out

from than someone who has lived with one for the best part of a decade.

Dave was brilliant and helped me separate all the crap from the stuff I really needed to know. I felt very overwhelmed with information and treatment options and it was good that I had Dave there to tell me which ones were worth pursuing.

Dave and Tom grew very close. They bonded over their tumours and the fact that no one else could relate to what they were going through. Tom always used to say that people would say to him, 'I can imagine it is hard what you are going through' but of course they couldn't. But Dave did. Tom would call Dave all the time. He would ask him for advice on diets and exercise but also symptoms, like if he felt a certain way after radiotherapy or if he was having headaches.

As well as Dave, I spoke to healers about the power of the mind and looked into reiki, a therapy which balances the flow of energy in the body. The reiki healer, or master, believes that negative areas of energy or blocked energy can build up to cause stress, tension, anxiety, or worse disease, so they work with the patient to remove it.

I also read a lot about our soul's journey and Tom's belief

that we live on, even when our bodies do not. It was all total enlightenment for me. I felt like this wouldn't just be a way of life to cure Tom, but our new way of life altogether.

Tom lived a very clean life after his diagnosis – he drank filtered water from a special tap in our house and took herbal remedies as part of his treatment. He had medicinal cannabis to take away some of his pain, and when I saw the effect it had on him, and how much better he felt, I looked more into plant remedies and how they are used to heal people.

When you think that thousands of years ago there weren't any medicines or hospitals and everything was taken from plants, and how suddenly we've stopped doing that. I'm not suggesting people shouldn't use conventional medicine, absolutely not, but I really do think that alternative therapies and treatments can't do any harm and, in Tom's case, enhance any conventional treatment he was having.

Homoeopathy was something I looked into when I was researching treatments for Tom. It isn't just taking herbal medicines for physical ailments, but also to heal you mentally and emotionally. I liked the idea of natural remedies and their healing powers.

Since Tom has died I have adopted some of those

Stepping Out

therapies for myself. I still have the filtered water tap and if I have a cough or cold, I go to Tom's homoeopath before I go to the pharmacy. I have had a huge lifestyle change. For me, it's about preventative measures and keeping me and the kids healthy. It took something bad to happen for us to have that shift in our lifestyle. With that in mind, I was ready to share all my knowledge and learnings with other sufferers, so I called Giovanna. 'I'm in,' I told her.

Giovanna had also roped in Vicky Pattison, Pete Wicks, Candice Brown and a new, up and coming Tik Tok influencer called Dr Emeka Okorocha.

When we arrived in North Africa, I met up with my team who were amazing. They all had their own stories and reasons for being there and I was excited to spend the next week or so with them. There were over 100 of us on the walk raising money for the breast cancer charity CoppaFeel!

I knew it would be gruelling, walking 10 hours a day, but that's the point of a charity trek. You need to put your mind to it and then you'll be fine.

It wasn't something you could train for as the terrain is so different to anything here in England, I just had to use my mental power to get me through and pray my legs wouldn't give up on me. It was just incredible. I needed a challenge for this year and thought there's nothing bigger than trekking the Sahara. It's something I'll always have in my heart and a memory I'll always treasure.

It was emotional because I had people in my team who had stage four cancer, and I had lived with someone who had stage four cancer for 18 months. I remember looking at one of my team one day, and thinking, 'If she can get through this, I can get through this, and we can get through anything.'

There was one man who had lost his wife three years earlier to breast cancer. He had a daughter and I asked him how old she was now, three years on. It was so nice to hear from someone who has been through something like me, and to know that one day, we will feel OK again. My kids are going to be at that stage after losing their dad and we spoke about the road ahead, like the kids going to school. I can't talk to everyone about that because they don't know what I've been through or what I am going through. But he actually understood it all and how I felt.

The trek was mentally challenging. It's hard for me to say that, because some of these people were living with cancer, but I was their leader and I felt the responsibility to

Stepping Out

keep their spirits up and to make sure they got through it. That we got through it together.

Physically it was also hard. One minute we were walking across sand, and then rocks. They were so hard and painful under our feet – it would hurt so much and you would pray for flat ground again.

We would walk and could see camp in the distance, but it was just a mirage. We thought we were so close, yet we would walk five hours straight to get there. It was definitely really hard but there was not one point where I thought I should give up.

I definitely felt Tom was with me on the trek. Every step of the way.

Ultimately I did it for him. I pushed myself out of my comfort zone to get the message out there about cancer. It was such an achievement for me, and the first time since Tom had died that I actually felt proud of myself, that I had actually achieved something. It gave me such a buzz and a high – I guess it was the first time I felt elated since Tom. The first time I've actually felt something that isn't emptiness or loneliness or just nothing at all.

There was one moment in particular when I really felt Tom's presence.

With And Without You

When he died I had told the kids that Tom had gone to be with the angels and the butterflies, so when a butterfly flew past me as I got to the top of a sand dune, I very much knew it was Tom.

I bet he was saying something like, 'Hi babe, only me, you are mad doing this you are, but I am so proud of you!'

DECEMBER 2022

25th First Christmas without Tom

10

The Greatest Gift

'Tom loved everything about Christmas but this one was going to be the best yet'

The first Christmas without Tom was much harder than I could ever imagine. This time last year, we were in our new home, our first Christmas there, and now I was finding myself wrapping presents on my own. The hardest part was writing gift tags just from me. 'To Rae, to Bo, Merry Christmas, Lots of love Mummy'. It doesn't look right. I mean I don't think Tom wrote a gift tag or wrapped a present in his life, but that's not the point is it? He can't now, even if he wanted to. I never wanted someone to come into the room and start helping with the wrapping more than at that moment.

The start of December 2022 was the coldest it had been in a while and we had snow and ice as we prepared for Christmas. That was tough in one sense because it brought back bittersweet memories. Tom loved the snow. He would've been getting the kids up early, buying the biggest sledges and finding the best slopes to race down! It's sad the

The Greatest Gift

kids will miss out on doing all these things with their dad, sometimes that's the hardest part. Not what I've lost but what the kids have lost.

To be entirely honest, if I didn't have children, I think Christmas that first year without Tom would have been cancelled. I was dreading every moment of it – the food shopping and picking up his favourite drink, Jack Daniel's, and then putting it back on the shelf, laying the table and not having a spot for Tom. But I had to get through it for the children. Christmas is all about the kids and they were excited. They had always been my reason for getting out of bed and I needed to be strong for them now more than ever.

We spent the day at our house with my family. It was another first for us as we were always at my mum's but I couldn't bear to go. Tom had spent Christmas Day at my mum's every year since we met, bar one, and I couldn't bring myself to be there for that first one without him. I couldn't go to where Tom had his last Christmas.

We still had a Christmas dinner with all the trimmings, a few jokes, games with the kids, but it obviously wasn't the same. Tom's absence was massively felt. The chair he would have sat on was empty and I would have done anything for him to be sitting there seeing the kids tuck into their dinner and rip through their presents.

We were also missing another important man in our lives. Just weeks before that first Christmas without Tom, I lost my grandad, Peter, to leukaemia. What a shitter of a year it had been.

I was so close to my grandad, who was my mum's dad, and it broke my heart. He was like a dad to me and my brother Sammy and he raised us like we were his children. He shared so much wisdom and knowledge with us, and he would always make sure we were on the right path in life. He supported us in everything we did and applauded our achievements. He was so proud of his family. And we were proud of him, he was our hero.

But now another grief journey was about to begin.

My grandad's health had been up and down for some time. Just after Bodhi's first birthday he had a stroke. It's funny because Tom, who at that time was with us and battling his own health, was Googling ways to recover after a stroke. Dr Google at it again! He looked up what foods he should eat, what exercises he should do. I think it gave Tom something else to concentrate on that wasn't his own cancer. He adored my grandad, he'd do anything for him.

The Greatest Gift

My grandad was really affected by Tom's death. They were so close – Tom was like another grandson – and I think Tom dying broke him. Not that he'd ever say as much. He was quite an insular man and I say that not as a criticism, but he just liked who he liked and did what he wanted to do. I guess that's where my mum gets it from. But when I introduced him to Tom in our early days of dating they got on like a house on fire. It was the start of a beautiful relationship.

My grandad was such a caring and funny soul and he had the best laugh, it was so infectious. It was very hard for us as a family to see him unwell.

By July 2022, four months after we had lost Tom, we celebrated my nan's 80th birthday. 'Oh this is amazing,' I thought. My grandad walked in and it was the best I'd seen him look in a long while. Then later that summer we all went on a camping holiday, me, the kids, my mum, Johnnie, and my aunt Ju and uncle Danny and Nan and Grandad too. We really enjoyed it. It was the first time I felt able to smile in a long while.

But weeks later, my grandad took a turn and he was diagnosed with leukaemia. The doctors told us that while adults do get leukaemia – a cancer of the bone marrow and the lymphatic system – the strain my grandad had was more common in children. It was super rare.

I couldn't believe it. Tom's cancer was also rare, and now my grandad has been diagnosed with a cancer more common in childhood.

Chemo wasn't an option given his age and the type of cancer. Even if he was given it, I don't think he would have lasted. I think it would have killed him because he wasn't physically strong enough for it.

It felt like a huge blow. Life was still very much a blur at that time after losing Tom, and now as a family we had to go through it all over again.

By the end of November, my grandad had really deteriorated and he sadly died on December 2nd, almost nine months to the day since we lost Tom.

I wish I could say my grandad had a peaceful death like Tom did, but it wasn't to be that way. Their deaths were very different. Tom's was very peaceful, whereas my grandad tried to fight it and was in pain. I do wonder if it's because my grandad didn't have that spiritual belief. Tom's soul was ready to go, even if his body wasn't until the very end. But with my grandad, I feel like his body and soul didn't want to go, he wasn't ready to go, or maybe he hadn't accepted

The Greatest Gift

he was dying, and I think that made his exit from the world all the more painful. In truth, I think he was scared, whereas Tom wasn't in the end.

Looking back now, my grandad did change in the last few years. He had been in the war and had been through so much in his life, like losing his son. He was so strong and resilient. But I think that the pandemic made him withdrawn. I think he became scared to go out. All of the 'Don't kill your granny or grandad' messages really scared him and he was as terrified of COVID as if it was a cancer. I really do think that's why in the end he was so worried and full of fear.

His funeral took place on December 23rd. It was another really tough day. I read a poem and I am not sure how I did it because I was practising it the day before, wanting to make my grandad proud, and it absolutely tore me apart. The only comfort I had going into that first Christmas I was dreading so much was that my grandad was up there with Tom and my Uncle Neil, all sharing a bottle of red wine.

On what we now know was Tom's last Christmas, he was feeling happy and healthy. We had not long moved into our new family home and for the first time in a long time we felt there was some normality in our lives again. Tom's tumour was stable and we were both over the moon. He said it was an amazing Christmas present, and the only one that could have beaten it would be if the doctors had said it was completely gone. But we were so grateful that the tumour was stable as it's such an aggressive disease and to be where he was after 16 months was amazing. I think even the doctors were stunned.

It meant that Tom was able to do more things with the children – like getting up and making their breakfast. He couldn't do that while having treatments as he was too weak.

'I feel like I am part of the family unit again,' he said to me. For me, Tom had never not been part of the family unit, but I guess for him there were times when he felt isolated and unable to enjoy the things he wanted to with me and the kids.

In contrast, I remember Christmas 2020 was a difficult one. It was Bodhi's first so we tried to make it as special as possible, but Tom wasn't himself. He had not long been diagnosed and was recovering from intense rounds of chemo and radiotherapy. He was far from being the life and soul, helping my mum in the kitchen and singing and dancing. We had stayed at my mum's the night before and Tom

The Greatest Gift

was so exhausted I think he spent the whole day in the chair in his dressing gown. I don't even think he ate his Christmas dinner as he felt so sick.

Tom was determined to make Christmas 2021 a different one and he looked and felt like a different person. He was so excited for that Christmas – Tom loved everything about Christmas but this one was going to be the best yet. By this point he had lived with his tumour for 16 months and we were feeling positive about his outlook.

We were spending Christmas at my mum's again, like we always did. We woke up at home, it was me, Tom and the kids and they were so excited, especially Rae. Tom and I had bought them a massive trampoline so they went out on that cold Christmas morning in their pyjamas and coats and were happily bouncing on it.

Then we headed over to my mum's and we watched the kids tear through more presents before we all sat down and ate together. I remember we all watched a film, *Home Alone*, and Tom even had a couple of beers. We didn't know it would be Tom's last Christmas, but if we did, we wouldn't have changed a thing about that day.

Tom never spoke about 'lasts' and neither did I. I am sure there might have been a moment during that Christmas where it crossed his mind that it might be his last, but then I think he would have quickly snapped out of it.

He put so much work and effort into getting to the stage he was during that Christmas that there was no way he was going to give it all up now. 2022 was about carrying on the fight.

Tom had been on immunotherapy treatment, something we couldn't have done without the help of friends and family. It worked by starving the blood in the tumour to stop it growing. At £3,000 per treatment, every couple of weeks, it was crippling us.

It was so touching that Ed Sheeran offered to pay for the treatment. Tom and Ed had known each other since they shared a tour bus in America around 10 or so years earlier and they had stayed in touch, bumping into each other now and then at industry events.

Anyway, Ed ended up paying for the lot. I won't embarrass him by revealing how much the bill was because he has never publicly spoken about it, and people only know as Tom thanked him in his book, 'Hope'. But all I can say is we were so grateful to Ed. I still am. He really didn't have to do that for us, and those vital treatments that we couldn't get on the NHS gave us precious more months with Tom. Who knows

The Greatest Gift

how many, it doesn't bear thinking about, but I'm sure it was a lot more than if he didn't have it. Ed's gesture essentially kept Tom alive and that makes him a very special man.

It's funny because I was watching Ed's documentary on TV recently and was thinking about Tom. It was very moving, and Ed discussed his own wife's cancer battle, which came after Tom died. It was the type of thing Tom would have loved to watch and it made me sad that he wasn't there. I just wanted to dissect it all with him. I have moments like that where I think. 'Tom would have loved this', then feel sad that he is missing out on so much.

As 2021 came to an end, we were hopeful about the future. Tom had even been saying he was broody and he would have loved more children. We toasted to the new year – wishing this would be the year Tom was cancer-free, with hopefully more babies and positivity.

New Year's Eve in 2022 without Tom was just incredibly hard. They say that it can be a lonely time of year anyway, and it's impossible to describe the intense feeling of loss you experience when the clock strikes midnight and the person you rang in the last 15 years with isn't there anymore.

I was talking to my friend over Christmas about the

sudden, empty feelings of grief that hit me from nowhere. I told her that the only way to describe it was like a wave flooding through your body, a surreal emotional awareness that Tom is no longer here.

This sounds wrong but it's almost like when you lose a set of keys. Do you know how you get that first feeling and you think 'where are my keys?' – it's almost like that and you think, 'Where is he? Where is he?' Your brain is in a temporary state of disbelief. I have to reassure myself and the conscious part of my mind resets itself, to remind me that he's not coming back and I have to resolve myself to that brutally sad truth.

Sometimes I have that maybe five times a day. But then life continues and ultimately I'm a mum, so the day to day reality of that overtakes my thoughts. Aurelia had me up four times last night – it's like I'm back to having a newborn. She just needs to be on the go and doing stuff. She is her father's daughter and I don't think she's stimulated enough so at night she's like, 'hey Mum, let's have a party!'

JANUARY 2023

1st Starting a new year without Tom

11

Gold Forever

'As we start a new year, I hope that one day I will be able to listen to Tom's voice again and not feel the pain I feel now'

It's January 2023, and it feels very different from this time last year. People often make resolutions on New Year's Day – goals, ambitions, achievements. I just hope I have a better year than the last. Getting through a day without feeling sad would be an achievement. Looking back, I do think I have come a long way mentally. I think the trek in particular was a turning point for me, and a place where I felt I healed a bit.

Tom and I started 2022 with so much hope. After 18 months or so since his diagnosis, things started to feel a bit calmer for the first time. A bit more normal.

One of Tom's dreams was to live in a million pound house. That probably sounds a bit big-headed or cocky, but trust me, when you live in south east London, a million doesn't go that far, ha ha.

Tom had set his eyes on a house about five minutes away from our old house, but bigger. It had more bedrooms and a

Gold Forever

space for him to make music – practically his own recording studio.

As soon as we went to view it, we knew it was our forever home, that's what Tom called it. It had a fake wall which looked like a bookcase that behind it revealed a downstairs shower and utility room. We also had a spare room in the attic and a dressing room for me, well, and a bit for Tom. He had quite a lot of clothes for a boy.

Tom really believed we would grow old here together. He said it himself. We didn't know what was going to happen with his health over the next few years, but all that mattered to Tom at that point was that me and the kids were happy and Rae and Bo had a lovely home to grow up in.

I don't think there are a lot of people out there who would move house during treatment for cancer. After all, they say that moving is one of the hardest and most stressful challenges you can go through in life, along with grief and divorce, but I think that for Tom buying the house represented a new beginning for him. For us. He was so proud of himself and life there felt like a new chapter.

Speaking of chapters, Tom paused his book writing while he rehearsed for The Wanted tour. They were due to start their tour in February and Tom couldn't wait. But first we had to get him over to Spain for a 20 day-programme at the clinic. Tom was trying a new immunotherapy treatment not available in the UK. It was called dendritic cell therapy which Tom was very excited about. It works by helping the body to create these antibodies that then go on to attack the bad cells, the cancer, basically. It isn't invasive like chemo and radiotherapies can be and is totally pain-free. It also has no side effects, which was a great relief to Tom. Sometimes the side effects were worse than the treatments themselves. The therapy also uses the body's natural healing system to kill cancer cells. If your immune system is at its healthiest, then the body should kill the cancer cells by itself. I remember someone comparing it to a clean pond; if you keep it clean then you will be healthy, but if you have algae and other things dropping in, you will struggle to keep that water clear. It's the same with the body. As well as the DCT therapy, Tom also had blood tests, oxygen masks, red light therapy and physio. They also looked after his diet.

Travelling for the treatment was almost like an all-inclusive holiday, but with a far more serious purpose, of course. It was expensive, just over £11,000 for a three week stay, but we knew for the results and the way he felt afterwards, it was worth every penny.

Gold Forever

While we were there Tom took to Instagram to update his fans:

'So as most of you know I've been out in Spain on a treatment programme for the past couple of weeks. It was only meant to last 20 days but due to a couple of logistical changes with tests and results it won't be complete until the end of the week now which has delayed our journey home. I'm obviously gutted that I'll be missing the first few shows (of the tour) but as I'm sure you will understand I have to complete my treatment cycle. I've been zooming into rehearsals all week and I know that the show will be incredible and that my boys will hold the fort until I'm back. Can't wait to see you all very soon, hope you all enjoy the show. Much love, Tom x'

His fans were incredible as they always were. For most of them it was their dream to have the five boys back together on stage and not having Tom there would have been such a shame for them, but at the same time they knew that health came first and they sent him so many lovely messages of support. It was just what he needed because he had really been missing the kids. We both had. It was the longest time we had ever been away from them. When someone has cancer, it affects the whole family and you have to make sacrifices. It was such a difficult decision for us to leave Rae and Bo for three weeks, especially as they were so little. Rae was only 19-months-old and Bo had just turned one. But we knew back home our family and friends would be there to look after them.

As well as my mum Di and aunt Ju in my support 'village', we also have Kelsey and Dean who have the kids whenever I need them to. Dean even ferried Tom around the country on the tour, taking him to every gig from Bournemouth to Liverpool. Since Tom died I have also had so many offers of help from so many people. In Bromley, where we live, it has a real tight-knit community feel. I grew up here so I know quite a few people, many who just want to help.

By the time we eventually got back from Spain – and had given the kids the biggest kiss and cuddle – Tom was feeling good and in the best possible health to go on that tour. He couldn't wait. He loved performing and he loved being back on stage with the boys. He had missed the first few gigs in Glasgow, Newcastle and Leeds, but he made it to Bournemouth on March 7th, which was my birthday.

When I look back now I do feel a bit sad that I didn't

get to spend my birthday with him. I obviously didn't know it would be the last one with Tom at the time. But on the other hand, Tom was doing what he loved, and I knew it made him so happy to be back on that stage. That was my birthday gift from him – to see that he was so happy.

When Tom arrived at Bournemouth to join the band for that first gig, I think they were worried about Tom being OK to perform. A lot of effort had gone into making sure the stage was safe and that Tom had somewhere to sit if he needed it. One of the effects of cancer is that it makes you very tired, and as Tom had brain cancer, it also affected his mobility meaning he couldn't stand for long periods of time.

It was arranged for a chair to be put into the centre of the stage so Tom could join the boys for the last song of the gig, *Glad You Came*. The chair, which was actually a throne, would rise up to the stage with Tom on it, and then the boys could join him. I think the band were a bit nervous about it. Would it be too much for him? Will it be too loud? Too bright?

'He's going on,' Dean told the production team. 'He wants to go on and he's going on,' and I think Dean practically chucked him into the throne. There was no way Tom was going to be at the gig and not get the chance to be on the stage.

As the show came to a close, with one more song to go, Max, Nathan, Siva and Jay welcomed Tom to the stage. Nathan said, 'Give it up for Tom Parker' and the crowd went wild. Nathan then said, 'As you guys can probably tell there is a massive space in this band tonight. And we love Tom as much as you do.

'In fact, we'll be big-headed and say that we love him slightly more, which is a lot. We can't wait to have him back which will be very soon. He sees all your messages and everything.'

Tom decided to wear glasses on stage because he obviously thought of himself as a bit of a rock star. It was also there to protect his eyes from the lights. As you can imagine at any gig, there are lights flashing around the arena and Tom was quite sensitive to that.

After the gig, the band's official Twitter page posted a picture of the five of them on stage and wrote, 'Like the king that he is! The f***ing legend that is Tom Parker. Bournemouth that was so special!!!' Tom would have bloody loved that, being referred to as a king!

Gold Forever

Tom then travelled with the boys on to Brighton, Cardiff, Nottingham, Birmingham, Manchester, Hull, London and Liverpool. While in Manchester, Max shared a video of Tom under a blanket with a bottle of beer. He was definitely living his best life on that tour!

Other pictures started to emerge of Tom as his eyes started to close. If I am honest, I found it quite distressing to see that. He was so far away from home and I hated that he was starting to change. Was he in pain? Did his eye hurt him? I wanted to get him to the doctor to see if it would reopen. Fans also began to comment on his appearance. Luckily Tom didn't see any of it, but I did. Nothing was ever said with malice and I know harm wasn't meant, but obviously people commenting on the fact they thought Tom looked frail and weak was very hard for me to read.

Back then, we obviously didn't know that Tom was in his final weeks, but even if he had known, he still would have gone on that tour. He wanted to be back with the boys so desperately and hoped it would be the start of a comeback for them.

Sadly that wasn't to be.

Jay has since said that the boys won't tour ever again now Tom is no longer with us.

With And Without You

'I'm not sure it would work without Tom,' Jay said. 'It just wouldn't feel the same. We will be doing some one-off shows early next year to help raise money for The Brain Tumour Charity – but I don't feel ready to tour again, and naturally that's a lot to do with losing Tom.'

He added, 'I think anything like [death] does bring people closer. We always stayed close and supported each other, even when we decided to go our own ways. But after Tom went, it gave us all another level of perspective about what matters in life. He was so loved, and we all miss him. I wish he had more time.'

I think Tom's music career will be a great source of comfort for the kids in the future. It's not the norm, is it? When other people die, kids don't get things like that, they don't get a record that says that their dad sold five million copies of something, they don't get to watch videos of him in interviews or playing music to thousands of people.

To this day I still can't listen to Tom's music, be that songs from the band, or his own tracks he recorded at home. I'm not ready for that yet, and I'm not sure I will be. I can't watch old videos of Tom either, or hear his voice. It's just still too raw for me. There's one song in particular called *Gold Forever* where Tom opens the song with the line, 'Say my name like it's the last time. Live today like it's the last night'. I've never ever realised it before, but when he died I recognised it. I actually can't believe the pain in the lyrics that Tom sings. And that's really hit me and now I think that I struggle to listen to his music even more.

As we start a new year, I hope that one day I will be able to listen to Tom's voice again and not feel the pain I feel now. But at the moment it brings me too much trauma. It's one of the grief hurdles I haven't been able to get over yet. But I will.

FEBRUARY 2023

14th Valentine's Day

12

The Future

'After all this grief and heartache, I hope one day I might get a bit of happiness. Tom would not want me to be sad'

Undoubtedly, the most romantic thing that Tom ever pulled out of the bag was probably when he proposed to me. I was 26 and Tom was 28 so we were quite a few years into our relationship. Even still, it totally came out of the blue for me.

The Wanted had come to an end two years earlier in 2014 after a fall-out during their reality show. They had been in America the year before filming The Wanted Life with their new manager Scooter Braun – who was behind the success of Justin Bieber – but I think it all came to a head and a few of them ended up at loggerheads. Typical Tom felt in the middle of it all, and when the band were no longer a thing and they all went their separate ways, he didn't know what to do with himself. Actually, that's a bit of a lie, Tom wanted to do everything, but he couldn't decide what to do first!

Tom lived his life at 100 miles per hour, and if he did

The Future

something, he would put absolutely everything into it. He would take it seriously. So when he was offered to take part in Channel 4 reality show The Jump in 2016, Tom seized the opportunity with both hands.

'I am going to be good at this,' he told me. And I didn't doubt him for one second. Tom wasn't just good at everything he did, he was amazing.

For those who don't know, The Jump involved celebrities taking on various winter sports such as skiing, bobsleigh and skating. Every episode, the two celebrities who recorded the slowest speeds had to do a live ski jump to keep their place in the competition.

Tom actually went in as a back-up originally, which obviously annoyed him as he was raring to go. But it was the year when sadly almost half of the contestants got injured. Gymnast Beth Tweddle fractured two vertebrae and needed surgery on her spinal cord after colliding with a barrier; Linford Christie had a hamstring injury; Sarah Harding damaged her knee; Rebecca Adlington dislocated her shoulder and Made In Chelsea's Mark-Francis Vandelli fractured his ankle.

Then, when Tina Hobley sadly dislocated her elbow, it was Tom's turn to appear on the main run – much to my reluctance. I was terrified he was going to get injured too. But Tom absolutely loved it and had the time of his life out in Austria for three months. He formed close friendships with James Argent – Arg – and Rebecca, and both of them are still in touch with me now.

It made me feel so much happier knowing he had met friends there and was enjoying himself because I couldn't be there all the time. A lot of the celebrities' partners went out there to stay with them, but I couldn't do that as I was acting at the time.

'All the other girlfriends are coming out, why can't you come and see me?' he would say. I knew he was upset, but he accepted I needed to work too. He was always supportive like that.

Tom was so good at skiing that he only went and made the final – of course Tom was going to make the final! – so I did end up flying out for the final week. Arg, who had left the show earlier, was also flying out so we went together. It was the first time I had met him and we hit it off straight away, mainly because he bought me a Nando's. I could see why he and Tom had become mates.

When we got out there, Tom introduced me to Sarah Harding, who was in the room next door, Brian McFadden

The Future

and Louisa Lytton. I think they all quickly realised that if they were going to stay friends with Tom after the show then they would have to come through me as Tom was absolutely useless at staying in touch with people. Louisa was someone both Tom and I grew close to and stayed in touch with long after the show ended. In fact, I feel like Tom and Louisa were always meant to meet as they went on tour together in *Grease* for over a year, and I am not sure many other people would have put up with him for that long!

Tom did himself proud in the final – he finished in third place (out of an original field of 16) behind Dean Cain, aka Superman, and rugby legend Ben Cohen. He was well happy with that.

After the show ended there was a reunion where we all went out together in London. There were loads of us out that night, Lydia Bright was there with her then boyfriend Arg, and it all got a bit messy. I drank so much. It was stupid of me really, as the next day Tom was driving us to Chewton Glen in New Hampshire for a couple of romantic nights away.

'We haven't spent that much time together recently, so I have booked a trip away,' he told me.

'Really?' I replied.

'Yeah, I missed you when I was away so I thought it would be nice.'

Tom wasn't always the most romantic of people. I remember for my first birthday together he bought me a box of Ferrero Rocher. He had literally left it to the very last minute, ran into the nearest shop and grabbed what he could. I never let him live it down.

So when he said he'd booked this posh hotel, I thought he had really pulled out the stops.

Getting into the car that morning, I was probably green. I felt so rough. It was going to take us two and half hours to get to the hotel and I was dreading the journey.

We were about an hour into the journey – I had already scoffed a McDonald's to try and soak up some of the alcohol – when Tom turned to me.

'Did I put my laptop in my bag?' he said to me, looking a bit panicked.

'I don't know Tom, did you?' I replied. I really didn't care if he had his laptop or not. It was the least of my worries.

'I need to stop and check,' he said. 'If I haven't got it, we need to turn back.'

'We are absolutely not going back for your laptop Tom,'

The Future

I told him. Was he joking? There was no way we were going to make this journey any longer. And what was the bloody fascination with the laptop?

'I have got to send a track off, Kels,' he said.

'Are you having a laugh? No we can't go back,' I said, unimpressed.

Tom pulled over and started rummaging around in the boot. *Bang!* The boot closes.

'It's OK, I have got it,' he said, looking all pleased with himself.

'Well, thank God for that,' I said. And with that we were back on the road.

Arriving at Chewton Glen, I was blown away. It was absolutely amazing. We checked in and they took us to our room.

'Oh my God,' I said to him. 'You have got us a treehouse!' It was pure luxury. They looked like big, round villas sat up in the middle of the trees, and the interiors were five-star hotel quality.

'Done well, haven't I?' he joked as he gave me a hug.

Tom said we needed to get ready for dinner, so we got dressed and made our way down to the hotel bar. I remember being desperate for a large glass of ice-cold Coke to help get rid of the last bit of my hangover. By this point, Tom was starting to act a bit weird. He was so chatty, you couldn't shut him up, but he was a bit too quiet. He also made a weird comment about my nails saying that he liked them. Tom had never commented on my nail polish before. But even then, I didn't ever predict what was about to come next. Probably because I was still nursing my hangover from the night before.

After dinner we were driven back to our treehouse, and as I opened the door I saw all of these petals and candles on the floor. It was so romantic.

And then there was his laptop – the bloody laptop we almost had to go back for – sat on the side.

He hit play and it was a picture montage with a song written for us by my friend RuthAnne playing over it. It was just stunning. At the end, it said, 'Turn around' and as I did, Tom was there, down on one knee. It was so romantic.

'Do you know how much I love you? I wouldn't want to be with anyone else. Will you marry me?' he said to me with a smile and I could see tears in his eyes.

I screamed. 'Oh my God! Yes!' as I looked down at this beautiful diamond ring.

Then there was a knock at the door. As Tom opened

The Future

it, my mum and stepdad and Tom's parents walked in. 'Congratulations!' they said through huge smiles as they gave us each a huge hug.

My mum and Noreen took my hand and admired my ring. It was so shiny.

'There nearly wasn't a ring,' my mum laughed.

'What do you mean?' I said. Tom put his hand over his face, but I could tell he was smirking.

'I asked Johnnie if I could marry you,' he said. I didn't think I could love him more.

'But I didn't have a ring.'

'Your mum and Julie said he couldn't propose without a ring,' Johnnie said.

'So I went up to Hatton Garden and picked your ring,' he said as cool as anything. 'That was last week.'

I wasn't surprised by anything I heard. It was typical Tom. He wanted to propose, he didn't have a ring, but yet everything fell into place at the last minute.

'Were you not panicking, Tom?' his mum asked. 'Nah,' he said, and we all laughed.

'Oh, and Kels, I have another surprise for you,' he continued. 'Hello are doing an engagement shoot with us,' he paused before blurting out, 'tomorrow!'

'Tom!' I said, 'you bloody let me stuff my face with a McDonald's!' But how could I hold that against him? He had just pulled off a magical proposal which was absolutely perfect. And he'd even organised a magazine shoot. He really outdid himself.

'Maybe being a wife won't be so bad after all,' I thought.

Now, it's Valentine's Day 2023 and another first without Tom. This time last year I was full of hope. We had been in Spain on Valentine's Day where Tom was having his immunotherapy. Back then I didn't know that I would have just over a month left with my husband. The love of my life.

On the first Valentine's Day without Tom, I remember feeling every emotion all at once – anger, loneliness, sadness, a massive sense of loss, but also, maybe strangely, some comfort and a small feeling of happiness that I got to spend 13 years with such a wonderful and kind human being. I was lucky to have known and married Tom and I needed to remember that.

One of the worst things about being a widow to two young babies is definitely the loneliness. When Tom died, everything felt very empty and very quiet – in my heart but also in our home. My evenings became longer. I would try

The Future

and kill time, but essentially I was putting off the inevitable – getting into bed alone and without Tom. I often sit and eat on my own and after the kids are in bed, the house falls silent. It's horrible. I miss us curling up on the sofa watching crap reality TV or having a cuddle and watching a film. On this Valentine's Day without Tom, I suddenly felt very, very alone.

Except that's not what the papers were saying. 'Tom Parker's widow Kelsey looks happy as she's seen for the first time with new boyfriend' screamed one headline. Another read, 'Tom Parker's widow Kelsey looks happy as she's seen for first time with new boyfriend Sean Boggans'.

It's true that I had met someone, but I wouldn't have called him my boyfriend. It is hard to really describe my relationship with Sean given all that I've been through. It wasn't like some romantic film where he swept me off my feet and we ran off into the sunset and I forgot I was ever married to Tom. Far from it. But no one really wanted to hear how I felt.

Sean and I first met at his cousin's wedding in the summer of 2022. A couple of months earlier, just seven weeks after I had lost Tom, I had attended RuthAnne's wedding where I was her bridesmaid. It was one of the hard 'firsts' without

With And Without You

Tom. He should have been at that wedding with me, and his absence that day felt so huge. Tom was the life and soul of any party and I know he would have loved to have been part of the day. Tom loved a party more than anybody, but he especially loved a wedding. If he was there he would have been up on the stage, singing on the mic and first on the dancefloor. That was Tom's love for life and fun. He was so full of spirit – sometimes literally!

RuthAnne was amazing that day. She shouldn't have been worrying about me, it was her big day, but as my best friend she knew how hard it was for me to be at a wedding, a day full of love and promise, without my own love.

She arranged for an empty chair to be placed next to me during the ceremony, and on the back was a sign which simply read 'For Tom'. It was so special. Tom would have loved that he had a chair right at the front. We all raised a glass to him during the reception and I remember thinking, 'I bet he is up there doing shots.'

I won't lie, it was a tough day for me. Watching my best friend marry her soul mate when I have just lost mine was very bittersweet. Watching them making their vows to be together forever, to look after each other, love each other, 'til death do us part. But I was also so happy, RuthAnne

The Future

looked beautiful and radiant and happier than I had ever seen her. I was so honoured to be by her side.

When I got invited to my friend Zoe's wedding that September in Greece, I felt less apprehensive about it. I felt like I had got through my first wedding without Tom by myself, the singleton at the table, the one without a 'plus one' and felt that I could do it again.

The holiday was a much-needed break too. I'd thrown myself into work and life had been really hectic so this was the first time I could let my hair down and have some fun. With my mum and Ju looking after the kids each night, I drank a lot and was on a mission to forget my troubles.

Looking back, I don't need a psychologist to tell me I was numbing the pain and trying to escape my reality but, even on holiday, doing that was harder than I thought. I was either surrounded by friends and family who were constantly checking on me and asking if I was OK or I was away from that safety net but in with a new crowd who just knew me as Tom Parker's widow. Everyone looked at me with pity and walked on eggshells around me, not knowing what to say.

I have never felt more alone in such a big group of people. Where Tom and I had always felt part of the young crowd – still up partying with my younger brothers and cousins – I felt like I was being pushed into the older crowd and I wasn't ready to spend every night having a few quiet drinks on the balcony.

I met Sean at the bar.

'Oh my God, look at my cousin over there,' I said to him. She was so drunk and it was making us laugh.

'Someone's had a bit too much to drink,' he said to me.

'Haven't they just!' I said. 'I'm Kelsey by the way,' I told him.

'Sean,' he said. 'I'm Sam's cousin.'

We hit it off straight away, we just got on really well, chatting. It sounds silly but it felt like he was the first person not to treat me like a widow. I was due to fly back after the wedding to attend the NTAs where Tom had been posthumously nominated for his documentary Inside My Head, but due to the Queen's death on September 8th, the show had been pushed back, meaning I had an extra few days in Greece.

I really do believe everything happens for a reason, and on this occasion it gave me a bit more time to get to know Sean. All of Zoe and Sam's friends were staying on after the wedding and we all hung out together.

I liked that Sean had no idea who I was or anything

The Future

about Tom. He knew Tom had died, but he didn't know he was in a band or the circumstances.

It was a nice break to be honest. I had spent months of people asking me how I was, and how much they missed Tom, and being with Sean gave me a bit of respite. As much as my heart was broken and I missed Tom, it was so hard to keep talking about him. To keep reliving his diagnosis and death. In some ways, Sean gave me a bit of normality and time where I felt like I could breathe again.

I remember we were on the beach one day, and his friend said, 'You do know that's Kelsey Parker?' And he was like, 'Who is Kelsey Parker?' Sean was just a geezer who liked to go to the pub with his mates, the world of celebrity was totally lost on him, and it was nice.

It wasn't anything romantic at first, it started off as a friendship. I found Sean very easy to talk to and I picked up a nice vibe from him. As I say, he made me feel very normal and like Kelsey again. A few weeks later, when we got back to England, we talked some more and I met up with him. By this point, I could feel things were becoming more romantic.

Sean and I had things in common, he was also a dad to two little ones and we were both no longer with our partners, though obviously for different reasons. Sean had been split from his wife for some time, and I think when we met, we were both looking for someone to fill the void.

I can't say we began dating, because we didn't. It wasn't like we'd go on romantic walks or trips to the cinema, or have meals out. We would often find ourselves at home, cooking together and chilling watching TV.

Then he asked me if I wanted to go to a wedding with him in Greenwich. 'I won't know anyone,' I told him. 'It's all the same lot from Greece,' he said to me.

I remember feeling nervous about people seeing us together and speculating what this was. Tom's diagnosis to death might have been cruelly quick and everything over the last two years had been like a tornado but in more recent weeks and months, time had felt like it was standing still and everything was moving so slowly. I just felt so ready to escape it all and Sean gave me the chance to do that, but I wasn't ready to admit I was seeing someone else. I certainly wasn't ready for anyone else to know that. I was conscious of what other people would think, how others would be hurt but I wasn't ready to think about that and nor did I need to, so I put it to the back of my mind.

Sean was fine not to put a label on what we had and that

The Future

was important to me. I couldn't rush into anything new, or admit I had a new boyfriend and I didn't know or really care where it was going. I didn't need to look too far into the future. If Tom's untimely and tragic death had taught me anything it was to live for every day.

We ended up going to the wedding together and we had a brilliant day. It felt good to be around new and different people who didn't know my tragedy. I felt free and we had fun. I was momentarily escaping my reality and just being me again – a young woman having a good time at a wedding. It felt normal.

But the next day I got a call from my agent, Rachel.

She sounded different, she was confused and hesitant as she asked, 'Have you met someone?' Fuck. It's out. My heart hit my stomach.

'*The Sun* has sent a picture of you and a man at a wedding and it looks like you are kissing,' Rach said.

I tell Rachel absolutely everything, not only is she my agent but she is also my friend. Her opinion counts so much and I often ask her for advice. But I hadn't told her about Sean, for obvious reasons and I felt terrible she found out this way.

It was such a reality check. A reminder of everyone in

my life that would be affected by this new relationship or whatever it was. Rach had been there since Tom's death and we'd talked endlessly about my relationship with Tom, our love for each other, how we had met so young and were soulmates. Rach knew how I felt about Tom so I know she was flawed by this revelation and I was scared of what she and everyone else would think.

I told Rach the truth, that a few weeks earlier I met a nice guy at a wedding and we had seen each other a few times. I hadn't told her because I really didn't know myself what it was we had between us. At that point, I think I just wanted a bit of companionship if I'm being honest. I wanted a bit of male company, and someone to enjoy the evenings with. It would be unfair of me to say that I was using Sean to fill the massive hole Tom left in our lives because I did have feelings for him, but I wanted to take everything slowly.

'I understand, Kels, I get it' Rach said. 'I don't want you worrying about this, OK?'

I don't know what Rachel did, but *The Sun* ended up dropping the story. I think they understood the difficult circumstances and out of respect to Tom and I, they agreed not to run it and I really appreciated that. But, it was hard to

The Future

accept that someone was so quick to stitch me up and make a bit of money off a photo.

I had received so much love and support and then to realise how quickly that could turn. People are so quick to judge but it's true that we never really know what someone else is going through so we must be kind. That wasn't kind. At a time when my family and I were so vulnerable, to take that picture knowing what they wanted to do with it, to hurt us in the way it would, I felt quite violated and exposed and it was the first time I had regretted being so public with our journey. I felt judged and attacked and it forced me to have conversations with my friends and family that I just wasn't ready for. How could I tell Tom's parents that I'd met someone?

Weeks passed by, and I got another call from Rachel. '*The Daily Mail* now has the story,' she said to me. 'I don't think I can hold this any longer and I think it's time to prepare everyone for the story coming out.'

I called Sean straight away to warn him and within hours the news was out.

'Tom Parker's widow Kelsey 'finds love again' eight months after The Wanted star's death' was one headline.

But there was more to come. Sean had been very honest

with me from the beginning that he had been in prison. In 2013, he was involved in a fight where he knocked a man unconscious. The man sadly later died and Sean was arrested for manslaughter. He went on trial at the Old Bailey and was sent to prison for four years. It was the biggest mistake of his life and he will regret it forever. Unfortunately this story was too good for the papers not to print – 'Tom Parker's widow is shacked up with a killer'. It was the perfect tabloid story really, wasn't it? And the trolls were loving it too. Not only was I being bashed for 'moving on' and 'finding love' – their words, not mine – but I was also getting abused for dating someone who they saw was a criminal.

'Oh my goodness, if she knew about this side of him I personally would run a mile. She could do so much better. Don't think her husband would want the likes of him around his children. She deserves to find happiness but needs to look at the bigger picture' was one comment. Another read, 'Slightly worrying for her and her children, who are already grieving the loss of her husband and father, that her new boyfriend has spent several years in prison for manslaughter, seriously hope his temper has improved.' And they were probably two of the not-so-harsh comments. I felt so sorry for Sean. He didn't ask for any of this. He wasn't famous

The Future

or written about before he met me, and all of a sudden his private life is all over the papers and he is being painted as some aggressor.

People were so fixated on the fact Sean had been to prison that they were missing the point entirely. Everyone seemed to be up in arms that my grief had ended and I was over Tom. That meeting someone eight months after my husband's death was in their opinion too soon.

But what they imagined was happening couldn't be further from the truth. Yes, I had someone in my life but it didn't change how I felt about Tom and our marriage. Unfortunately, we can't put a time limit on grief, it stays with you till the day you die.

Yes, there are easier days, and Sean coming into our lives did make things easier for a while. He really took care of us when I needed someone to lighten the load for me. He is a very caring person and a strong man who in many ways did swoop in. Not to sweep me off my feet but to help with the practical things in the house, to make me smile and to keep me company and I'm incredibly grateful for that. It was a respite from the pain and I was glad to have it. I am a widow and I will grieve for Tom forever. I didn't forget Tom. And I never will.

With And Without You

I dreaded telling Tom's parents and brother Lewis, they were still in the depths of their own grief and now this. But as I should have known, they were brilliant. Noreen told me she wants nothing more than for me to be happy and it means the world to me that I have their support. Despite being initially hurt, Lewis even managed to make a joke of it, repeating the tabloid headlines to poke fun at me. It's such a reminder that none of this is a fairy tale, it's real life and we're all human. Finding the joke in all this is what we do as a family and nothing will ever change what we have.

And I know Tom would not want me to be lonely or unhappy. He wouldn't have objected to me having some company in the evenings. A bit of companionship. I never expected to be a young widow at my age, and Tom would have wanted me to live my life. He would want me to be happy. If the boot was on the other foot, there is no way I would want Tom to go through his life feeling sad and alone. I loved him too much for that. I would always, always want him to be happy.

I do wonder if people's judgement of me has undertones of misogyny. It seems that we expect female widows to stay alone and celibate forever. To wear black and to constantly be miserable and in mourning. Whereas men, we can't wait

The Future

to get them partnered up again quickly – a good woman to look after them will make everything OK again. They deserve that. Why is that? There are many famous male widows who have moved on, remarried and had more children with their new wives, and nothing is ever said about them. And it shouldn't. I'm not saying they also deserve the backlash, far from it. They are entitled to every piece of happiness they can get. But why is it that women get so badly trolled? Why is it an issue for women and not men?

As the first anniversary of Tom's death was approaching, I agreed to do a magazine shoot to mark the first year without Tom.

My agent Rach was asked by the editors if I would answer a pre-approved question about Sean and I actually had no issue with it. We were still together at that point and I hadn't spoken about him on the record – everything that was already out there in the newspapers and magazines was from so-called 'sources' and not from us. I had always promised to be honest and real about my grief journey and I knew that being transparent about my relationship with Sean was important to that. Of everything I've tried to teach people about grief and overcoming adversity it was this; don't let anyone else's judgements stop you from doing what you need to do to get through it.

I wasn't going to make the interview about Sean, this was a shoot with my kids to celebrate Tom, to reflect on the past 12 months without him and that was always my reason for keeping the relationship out of the public eye – because I didn't want any of it to overshadow Tom. But I did think that it would be a good opportunity to address it finally. Rip off the plaster, so to speak.

My agent Rach said I'd be happy to answer a few questions about Sean but requested these were sent in advance so we could prepare short answers and ensure the overarching piece was about Tom and celebrating his life and his two children a year on from his passing. Knowing they were only allowed one or two questions, they chose to ask, 'Do you feel guilty about moving on?'

I knew that Rachel felt uncomfortable asking me the question and she reassured me I didn't have to answer it and we could ask them to take a different direction. But in many ways, this question was easier than any other. I knew the world expected me to feel guilt and in many ways, this gave me the perfect opportunity to apologise to the world for betraying Tom's memory by getting into this

The Future

relationship, but do you know what? I didn't feel an ounce of guilt and this was my opportunity to explain why.

After a second's silence I said to Rach, 'Guilty?! Do you know what Rach, I feel guilty about a lot of things, but not in the way I think that everyone expects me to feel,' was how I answered. 'What I am going through is not something I would wish on anyone – the strength it takes just to get out of bed every single day and stay positive, be Mum *and* Dad and face my reality.

'I'll take all the help I can get in battling through this. Anything that gives me a microsecond of relief from the agonising grief and sense of loss. Not just losing Tom, but losing everything we had built together and believed we were going to share for the rest of our lives. So no, I don't feel guilt.

'I question if it's right for me, my kids, my life. I question every single thing I'm doing and I feel guilty for just being here. But to ask if I feel guilty would suggest it's as simple as meeting someone else and moving on and honestly it couldn't be any further from that, so guilt is the least of my worries and emotions right now.'

Rach stayed silent and then just said, 'Kels, I couldn't have said it better myself. That's your answer.'

Sean and I continued to see each other up until March

With And Without You

2023 but after Christmas I was not in a good place. Despite my best efforts for the kids, Christmas was tough and then it was a string of events without Tom; Valentine's Day, Tom's anniversary, Mother's Day, my birthday. Staying positive got harder and harder and the more I was struggling, the closer Sean tried to get until I just felt suffocated. Angry and confused I just couldn't keep going.

'I need to be on my own,' I told him.

The first year without Tom had been so difficult. Much of it was a blur, much of it I felt numb and there were some bits that I don't remember. For so long I just needed someone there by my side but accepting that person would never be Tom, as I approached the first anniversary of losing him, I just wanted to be on my own.

While Sean is a lovely person and was really keeping me going and helping in every area of my life, overnight I just felt like I needed some space to properly reflect on the last year. And ultimately I knew it wasn't fair on Sean to ask him to stick around while I was so all over the place, not knowing if I was coming or going, or whether I wanted a relationship or not. Sean was hurt and confused, but I gave him no choice but to accept my decision and go.

A few months after we split up I saw Sean at a friend's

The Future

wedding and I must admit it was lovely to see him. It felt like a nice sense of familiarity. We talked about what we had been up to and there was no awkwardness. We have exchanged a few messages since, just being friendly.

What does the future hold? In truth, I really do not know. There was a time when I thought Tom and I would grow old together and be laughing in chairs next to each other with all our grandchildren around us. Obviously that is not going to happen now or ever. That's why I try not to look too far ahead anymore. I do not want any more of my dreams to be shattered. Instead I am going to live for today, be present for my children and be the best mummy I possibly can.

I hope one day I do meet someone else. I have no shame in saying that. The moving on question feels so taboo to some people but I am never going to have the love that I had for Tom, yet that's not to say I won't find a different kind of love. A love that is still happy and pure. Tom would want me to be happy and he wouldn't want me to live my life alone. And I'm self-aware enough to admit, I just can't be on my own. I never have been. Tom knew that about me and he would absolutely not want me to be sad. I am sure he would also want me to meet someone fun and silly like him, to be a good role model to our children. No one will ever, ever replace Tom. Not as a husband or a dad. There won't ever be another Tom. I won't ever meet anyone else like him, he was so unique and special. Tom has a very special place in my heart and he always will. He will always be our babies' daddy and I will make sure they will always remember him.

But after all this grief and heartache, I hope one day I might get a bit of happiness. We all deserve that in our lives, don't we?

Epilogue

Journey's End

It's early summer 2023 and I'm writing this final chapter of my book. It has been an emotional few months, and at times it's been hard to relive a lot of the trauma and heartache me, the kids and mine and Tom's families have been through over the last two years. We have all had different grief journeys. Noreen and Nige's will be different from mine as they have lost their precious son. I have lost the love of my life, my soul mate, my husband. Aurelia and Bodhi have lost their dad. All of our grief is different for Tom but we all have the same love for him. I have learned in the past 18 months that your grief will never, ever go away, you just have to learn to live around it. I am never going to forget Tom but I now have to live my life without him.

Are there times when I wish I had died with Tom? Yes, of course. But what would Tom want me to do? He would have wanted me to live my life and live it to the fullest.

Writing this book really has also been quite therapeutic.

Journey's End

and as I look back on the last two years, I'm really proud of what I have achieved despite everything. I can't believe I'm writing my own book, Tom would have loved this. He would have loved that I was using my platform as he intended, but also so proud that I actually did this. He celebrated all of my achievements.

Of course, Tom will never read this. But that was the plan, it was part of the journey. I know somewhere he is saying, 'Go on, babe' and then, 'Don't get higher than me in *The Sunday Times* list!'

There have been times while writing this with the help of my ghost writer Lisa when we have belly laughed recalling some of the things Tom has done over the years. It has been so lovely and has filled my heart with happiness to think about all of those precious and happy times we had together.

I am also feeling more hopeful about the future and that one day we will find a cure for glioblastomas. And all brain tumours. All cancers. I'm proud to say in the past year I've become a co-director and trustee of Ahead of the Game Foundation, the charity I mentioned which helped Tom so much during the last year of his life.

My aim is to work with its founder Dave Bolton to raise

awareness for brain tumours, get more funding into their research, and help as many families like ours that I can to get the treatment that helped Tom and that has kept Dave in that top two per cent of survivors. I still can't actually believe that brain tumours are overlooked for funding, despite the fact that they kill more children and adults under the age of 40 than any other cancer.

Earlier this year, *The Guardian* ran a story about how the government gave £15 million to brain tumour charities over the course of five years – their promise in 2018 was £40 million. If they had received the full funding then who knows what that would have meant for Tom and thousands of others who have lost their lives to the terminator of all tumours.

I really do think that the government needs to do more, there is no doubt about that, but I'm not going to sit back and just wait. I'm going to do everything I can to get brain tumours talked about at the same level we talk about breast cancer or cervical cancer, and to make people aware of the symptoms.

As a start, we've just organised a charity football match in Tom's honour at our local football club, Bromley FC, where almost 3,000 people came out to watch a bunch

Journey's End

of celebrities, including Harry Judd, Ryan Thomas, Strictly stars Neil Jones and Kai Waddington, Gogglebox star George Baggs, and Love Island's Nathan Massey, Casey Barker and Finley Tapp. We also had support from ex-professional players like Jermaine Jenas and Katie Chapman. Every single penny went to Ahead of the Game, and as I am writing this, we are looking at about £25,000, possibly more, raised. The money will do so much for the charity and provide more care and support for those who need it.

My dream is to open another clinic, a second clinic like the one Dave has up north, but in the south-east region to make treatment more accessible to people all over the country. My big, big dream is to open clinics all over the country and share the fantastic work that Dave and his team do in helping those with all types of cancer.

The Tom Parker charity match took place on Father's Day, it was our second one without Tom. Last year, Father's Day was one of the hardest days for us as a family. I think I was in survival mode and trying to get through each day at a time.

It was like an out-of-body experience during that time for me. I was just on the go all of the time, but not really absorbing day to day life, if that makes sense. I remember thinking that it was Tom's day and he wasn't here to celebrate with us and that was obviously very hard for me and the children.

It made me very aware that every year at school, while other children will be making cards and gifts for their dads, ours won't be able to give theirs to their daddy. And likewise Tom won't be here to open his presents and cards from the kids on the day that celebrates him and what an amazing daddy he was. I was determined to make this second Father's Day different. I made sure it was a celebration of Tom's life and also a day Aurelia and Bodhi can enjoy and not one to dread. It was their special day where they can remember Daddy.

I hope to make the Tom Parker charity game an annual event. It was so successful that we are already in talks for the 2024 match. On match day, it was forecast to rain, but the sun shone all day, it was only at full-time did the rain start to fall. 'Alright Tom,' I joked. 'You don't need to cry that it is over!' He would have loved what we put on. My dream is to grow it, make it bigger and better every year. Tom loved football and it was the right way to celebrate him.

Aurelia still asks me most days why she doesn't have a daddy. I have to continue to be very honest with her,

Journey's End

as I always have and always will be. She starts school in September and I know more questions will come and, as hard as it is, I need to be prepared for that. I know it will be hard for her to see the other daddies there with their children on their first day and hers won't be. But I also know that when we go on that first walk to school this September, Tom will be right by her side, feeling as proud of her as I am.

I do wonder what Tom would think of our life if he was still here. Would he be happy with the primary school I chose? What would he think of Aurelia's modelling photoshoots and their weekly swimming lessons? Would he like what I've done with our hallway? Would he like the transformation of our driveway and front door?

My heart will always be broken but as a person I will start to heal. I know I will always have good and bad days, but on those bad days I just need to try and remember to focus on the positives.

Aurelia and Bodhi will keep me going. Without them I don't know what I would have done. They give me the strength to get out of bed every day. They have kept the light switched on in my life.

As I bring this final chapter to a close, I am thinking

about the future, what's next and how do I move forward? I keep looking at my wedding rings and wondering how long I keep wearing them? The marriage will never end but they're a symbol that I'm married, that I'm someone's wife and taken. But I'm not. I'm no longer a wife, I'm on my own and somehow it doesn't feel right to still be wearing them. When is the right time to make that transition and stop wearing them?

There is never going to be a right time to do it. What I have learned in my grief journey is that there is never a right time for anything. Only when it is right for you. Am I ever going to truly be the Kelsey I was before I lost Tom? No, absolutely not. I'm not a different person. I have had to grow, I have had to learn, I have had to cope. But above all of that I have had to try and navigate life without the man who I thought I would be married to forever.

I feel as though I've come to the end of a journey with this book, like it's bringing me some closure and a pressure to start closing doors to make way for new ones opening. I feel like it is some kind of symbolism, like a fresh chapter in my life. Letting go of the life I was supposed to live with Tom is the hardest thing I will ever do, but being here, in no-man's land, not in my old life and not accepting my new

Journey's End

life, well this is like some kind of slow and silent torture and I know I need to get out of it. Maybe it is time to remove my wedding rings and move forward as Kelsey Parker, mum of two and widow? It does not mean I am forgetting Tom or removing him from my life, of course it doesn't. He is in my heart. Tom will always be part of my story, even though he won't now be part of my future.

I haven't decided what I will do with my rings in the future. I think I'd like Aurelia to have my engagement ring when she is older, and Bodhi can have Tom's ring. I might also get my ring made into jewellery like a necklace or something so Tom is close to my heart.

I just hope and pray that one day both Aurelia and Bodhi find what Tom and I had. I want them to marry their soul mate. I know that would have been Tom's wish too if he was still here.

Rae and Bodhi rely solely on me now and I have to make sure I am always there for them and that I give them the best life I possibly can. The life Tom wanted them to have. Tom had big dreams for them both. He built this future for us so we didn't have to ever worry. He didn't want them to struggle in life, financially, he made sure of that. It is now down to me to facilitate that. I have to make sure they meet all their dreams, goals and ambitions. They can be anything they want to be.

My kids are my motivation. I get up every morning and I go to work for them. I need to make sure that they have the best life possible. And I made a promise to Tom that they would.

I know I can't change what has happened to us. I know I have to accept this is our life now, and in some ways I already have. I have had to learn. But I promise I will use my platform to help others going forwards. Even in his darkest moments, Tom always helped other people. He was the kindest man with the biggest heart and so much love and for that he won't ever be forgotten. I feel like Tom gave me the gift of his platform when he left, and he would want me to carry on the work he started.

Tom had a huge platform, quite literally a stage. He had a platform as a singer, he had a platform once he was diagnosed, even when he did Stand Up To Cancer, he had a platform where he could raise awareness. Since his death, I've been given so many opportunities to continue his work, through media interviews, the audience I've built across social media and through the charity work I've done in his name.

My friend said to me, 'He took you on this journey so

Journey's End

you could continue his work, to help others. Tom fulfilled all he came here to do and now it's your time to take it on.'

Everything I've done in the past two years has been meaningful in so many ways. At first it was an opportunity to keep Tom's spirit alive, it was a much-needed distraction from the pain and silence of grief but it's slowly evolved into so much more. Helping others, making a difference, the sense of purpose and fulfilment I get from doing this is really very special. If I can make this my career, my purpose in life, the mark I will leave on this world then I'll be very happy.

One of the things I've learned about death during my grief journey is that despite the fact I've suffered the most traumatic experience in losing the love of my life, the world doesn't stop for me, it keeps on turning.

The sun still rises and sets and every day it keeps shining. And I know that Tom is watching over me every day, especially when the sun is on me. I can feel it and I can feel him. He may be physically gone from this world, but he will live on in my heart forever and what I do next doesn't change the past, but it matters for our family's future. I have to keep going. One foot in front of the other…

Afterword

By Dave Bolton

'There is another way, another option but most of all there is hope'

I first met Tom and Kelsey in 2020 when they got in contact through my charity Ahead of the Game Foundation.

Like Tom, I have a grade four glioblastoma. I was first diagnosed with a stage two Astrocytoma, an incurable brain cancer, after suffering a huge 15-minute seizure while sleepng in May 2014. It was so huge I had stopped breathing, dislocated my shoulder and bit through my tongue. Scans showed I had a tumour the size of a tennis ball at the frontal lobe of my brain. I had something called craniotomy and debulking brain operation, where part of my skull had to be cut open to take out the tumour and then be put back together again. At that point, doctors at The Walton Centre for Neurology in Liverpool gave me a life expectancy of five years.

Afterword

At the time I was working for Merseyside Police, but I had to quit the job I loved and take medical retirement.

My big loves were rugby and martial arts so I took my passion for sport and went to Leeds Beckett University where I completed my Strength and Conditioning qualifications, specialising in rugby and combat sports.

Then a year later, during a routine scan, the doctors found another tumour. It was smaller than the first, around the size of a walnut and this one was located in the central hemisphere of my brain. I was back in hospital having my second brain surgery and tests later revealed it was a stage four glioblastoma.

At this point, my previous prognosis was out of the window and I was given a life expectancy of three months or six to eight if I had treatment. It wasn't a time limit I was willing to accept.

I started a six-week course of radiotherapy and chemotherapy at the Clatterbridge Hospital for Oncology, Wirral, but during my final week of treatment I was admitted to a mental health hospital for four days where they realised I'd had a breakdown due to the steroids I was taking.

I still wasn't prepared to accept my prognosis so I started a six-month course of chemotherapy, this time double the strength of the previous cycle. By April 2016, I had survived longer than any doctor had expected and a scan showed there only to be a few cancerous cells left. To this day, as I approach eight years since my glioblastoma diagnosis, I continue to have regular scans that show no signs of cancer. I am in the five per cent of people who survive with this tumour for more than five years.

As Kelsey has said, glioblastomas are the most common primary brain tumour in young adults and children, with around 2,500 cases every year in the UK. Yet not enough is being done to improve those survival rates and there isn't enough money going into research and funding as there is other cancers. This is why I set up Ahead of the Game Foundation. I work with Anna Crofton, Associate Director of Nursing for Cancer, my executive assistant and Digital Marketing Manager Debbi Kruger, and Olga Semenko, a cancer rehabilitation specialist coach to help with rehabilitation for those with cancer. That is looking after their mental and physical health as well as offering financial support.

We use different alternative therapies and have onsite nutritionists and physios at our clinics. One patient we have was told in February 2023 that her tumour had grown and

Afterword

things were not looking good, but she has spent time with us on our programme and I am pleased to say in April her tumour was stable again. We are just trying to bridge the gap between what is on offer on the NHS and what isn't. My dream is for that to grow and for more options to be given to people like me and Tom.

I'm devastated Tom wasn't here with us for longer. He deserved to be. He had so much fight, hope and promise in him. We grew so close during the time I knew him – we bonded as only we know how it feels to be given that kind of diagnosis.

Kelsey was amazing and a real rock to Tom during his treatment. She did everything she could to make sure every option was available to him and that nothing was overlooked. She amazes me with the information and knowledge she has learned in just 18 months.

That's why I wanted her to be co-director and trustee of our foundation. She is so passionate about helping people with tumours like me and Tom, but also all cancers. She wants to help people, inform people, and let them know there is hope. It wasn't to be in Tom's case, but I know Kelsey has helped so many families over the past year, particularly parents of children with brain tumours, and she is determined to carry on his legacy to ensure they get the best care possible.

Kelsey has been through something no woman of her age should ever have to go through. Her strength is incredible and she amazes me how she has carried on. I know Aurelia and Bodhi give her so much strength and they are also part of Tom's legacy. Her dedication and commitment to change is so inspiring. She is using her platform for the greater good and I can't thank her enough for all she has done to raise tens of thousands for our charity.

She is one special lady and a credit to Tom's legacy. I just know he would be so, so proud of her. We all are.

I Am Ready
written by RuthAnne

It was always right in front of me

I never knew, never knew

Now your song's like a symphony

it makes me move, makes me move

So here I am standing in the crowd slowly waiting for you

So sing your song, sing it loud

I don't know how you got me

I'm dancing from the inside out

Head over feet, your touch I feel

and now we're dancing from the inside out

I'll let all your love be your applause

We don't need to say nothing but

Ooooh, I'm ready now

So sing it out

Slowly all the sounds I hear are getting through

'Cos your love, oh it plays on me

and it fills the room like I need it to

And without you everything would be oh so out of tune

Sing your song, sing it loud
I don't know how you got me
I'm dancing from the inside out
Head over feet, your touch I feel
and now we're dancing from the inside out
I'll let all your love be your applause
We don't need to say nothing but…

Oh, you're all around
I'm ready for what we found
sing your song, sing it loud
I don't know how you got me
I'm dancing from the inside out
Head over feet, your touch I feel
and now we're dancing from the inside out
I'll let all your love be your applause

We don't need to say nothing but
Ooooh

I'm ready now
So sing it out

Acknowledgements

To Aurelia and Bodhi, you are my world and I love you so much. Everything I do, I do for you both. You are my everything. You have both given me the light in the darkness and I don't know what would have happened if it wasn't for you both – you have given me love and strength and you are the reason I get up every day.

Daddy would be so proud of you both and I know he is looking down on you every day. He is always with you and I know that he will live on in your hearts forever. I can't wait to tell you all the stories about your daddy when you grow up. He was funny, silly, sometimes annoying – OK, a lot of the time! – but most of all he was the best daddy in the world and you were both his pride and joy. He loved you both so much.

To my mum, Di, and Johnnie. Thank you for everything you do for me and the kids. Thank you for always being there for me, for helping out, giving me advice, telling me when you think I'm wrong, ha ha! Thank you for always being there for Tom too. For your love, your guidance, your

Acknowledgements

bad jokes Johnnie, ha ha. Honestly, he loved you both so, so much. And I know how much you loved him too. You are both amazing people and I honestly don't know what I would do without you both. Love you both so much.

My big brother Sammy and little brothers Bobbie and Maxwel. You are all very annoying and you all drive me mad, making me wish sometimes I had a sister, ha ha, but jokes aside you are the best brothers a girl could ask for. I love you all.

To Ju, Danny, Olivia and Reece – Ju, you are a total diamond. I always say everyone needs a Ju in their life. There are not many people like you, you are always willing to do so much for others. You are the best auntie ever and I am so lucky you are mine. Rae and Bo adore you, especially your cooking ha ha, and we are all so lucky to have you in our lives. We love you, Danny, Olivia and Reece so much and we are so lucky to call you family.

To my Nanny Lynda, you are an amazing lady who I love and admire so, so much. You are such a strong person and I know I get my own strength from you. Thank you for always being there for me, for looking out for me, especially after Tom died, and for being the best great nanny to Rae and Bo. I love you so much.

With And Without You

Noreen and Nige, I just want to say a massive thank you for being the best mother and father-in-law ever. Thank you for always supporting and believing in me and for giving me your amazing and beautiful son

To Tom's big brother Lewis, his lovely other half Nat, and their adorable boys Theo and Jude, thank you for always being there for us. It makes me sad that Tom isn't here as I know he would be the best uncle ever! I know he is watching over the boys.

Rach Hardy, my agent and my friend. I couldn't have written this book without you believing in me and my story. Thank you for always having my back and being with me every step of the way. You put me first with everything and always have my best interests at heart. You have always listened when I needed an ear, and given me the best advice when I have needed it. I bloody love how deep we can get with our convos sometimes, if only the walls had ears! But I absolutely love how you always find a reason to do something – or not! You never do something without a cause or reason, you are not a 'throw it at all the wall and see if it sticks' agent. You care so, so much. You are the best in the business by far and I bloody love you and your beautiful family! Thank you for everything, Rach.

Acknowledgements

Scarlett Short, what can I say, you have been there with me from the very start. You've seen me grow from a little 20-something with my big acting dreams to now a proud mum of two carrying on Tom's legacy. Thank you so much for all your love and support, you mean the world to me and I am so grateful that you have always looking out for me and had my back. There are not many in the industry like you. Thank you for everything you do for me, hun.

And to the rest of the S Creative team – OMG, thank you, thank you, thank you! You are all so bloody amazing and work so hard. Emily, I have to give you special mention as you are a star. Thank you so much for putting up with me and making me look like I'm amazing at social media content! I love working with you.

To Lisa Jarvis. I truly believe you were the chosen one to write this book with me. As you know, I don't believe in coincidences and I really do believe that when Tom and I first met you at a random showbiz event in 2014, that it was written in the stars for us to work together in the future. And what a journey it has been babe. We have laughed, we have cried, and we have also organised a charity football match while writing this book. We did it! Though I don't know how as we have non-stop gossiped and chatted so much. Lisa's dictaphone is full of random chats – like my neighbour returning my dog Dolly after she escaped and ran out onto the road, chats with Sammy about building our new front wall and Aurelia recording herself about a million times!

Lis, you are not only my ghost writer, but you are now my friend. It's lucky that you love all my long-winded stories eh, ha ha!

Kelsey and Dean – you are both the best friends ever! You have been there for me and Tom every step of the way. Tom left you the responsibility of looking after me and what a job you have done. Thank you for always being there for me and my babies. I could not have got through any of this without you both. I love you both so much.

Jemma – thank you for being my longest serving friend and always being by my side. Thank you for always making me look my best even at the worst times. You have always been there for me - either with an ear or a make-up brush!

Damien Sanders, thank you for supporting me and Tom over the years, not only as Tom's manager but as one of his best friends. You did so much for us when Tom was diagnosed, helping us with treatments and Tom's care, and we won't ever forget that. Me, Rae and Bo love you.

Acknowledgements

To Ashley Tabor. Thank you so much for everything you have done for our family, but especially for everything you did for Tom. You made a 21-year-old's dreams a reality and I know Tom never forgot that. I too will forever be grateful for everything.

To all The Wanted boys. Thank you for always being there for Tom. Thank you for looking after him always and for making his final weeks the best they could have ever have been. He loved you all, his brothers forever. And Jay, I have to say you were so amazing in that final week of Tom's life and I won't ever forget how you dropped everything to come and be with him. You gave me strength when I needed it. Thank you for moving in and being our housemate for a bit! You have such a good heart and beautiful soul. And Siva, Tom would have bloody loved seeing you on Dancing on Ice. You know he would have wanted you to trip and fall so he could wind you up! Thank you for your performance for him, it was so special, and thank you for being there. Boys thank you so much, we love you all.

To Dave Bolton, you absolute legend! You gave Tom so much love, support and promise but most of all you gave him hope. You are an inspiration to so many people and I cannot wait to see what more we can do to bridge that gap in the NHS and get more treatments available for those suffering from cancer. Dave, you are a real life Iron Man and we love you.

Rosie – thank you for being 'the third wife' and giving us baby Tommy. He truly is a gift and I'm so honoured to have seen him come into this world.

Sacha – I love you, Sach. You are always there for me and are my voice of reason.

Evie Montilla – thank you for everything. For your positivity, for your vibe, and for being there for Tom at the end. You are pure magic.

To all my amazing friends, there is no doubt you share the most amazing qualities. You always have my back and make sure me and the kids are OK. You always check in on me and I know you are always at the other end of a phone. I talk about 'my village' and you are all a part of it. Each and every one of you has made this year bearable for me – I couldn't have got through it without your love and kindness. RuthAnne, Holly, Nicole, Emma, Louisa, Jeni, Annie, Zoe, Rachel, you are all my family. Thank you for being there for me through everything Jen. You came into my life to give me structure and organisation I love you.

To Connie, you are the strongest little girl I know. You

Acknowledgements

fight so, so hard and I promise I will be with you every step of the way on your journey. You are so young yet you show so much strength, you are an inspiration. And to Connie's mum Tina, you are amazing and your love and courage for your little girl is also inspirational. She's got this.

To our gorgeous George Fox who is no longer with us. Beautiful boy, I know you are up there somewhere with Tom and he is looking after you. You were only 13 and taken far too soon but I promise you your legacy will live on.

George died 12 days after Tom with his mum Louise, dad Jamie and his sister Issy by his side. George is just one example of children who are diagnosed with glioblastomas and we can't let any more of our children die in vain. George, we will continue to fight for you and for Tom, that is a promise.

To my new friends who I have met on my grief journey in the past 12 months. Thank you to everyone at WAY (Widowed and Young).

You do such amazing work, bringing people like me together every day. No one ever expects to be a young widow, but you do so much to provide support to people who find themselves in that heartbreaking situation.

With And Without You

To James Ryan, Denise-Palmer Davies and Will Palmer – I have only known you all for a few months, but all three of you have done so much to help me raise funds for Ahead of the Game Foundation and for that I am forever grateful. You all worked so hard to help me pull the Tom Parker Charity Match together – a little idea I had a few months ago that turned into something so incredible and bigger than I ever imagined, all thanks to you. Thank you for making it happen. Same time next year, yeah?

Thank you to Steve Hanrahan, Paul Dove, Rick Cooke, Christine Costello and Claire Brown at my publishers, Mirror Books. I can't thank you all enough for giving me a platform to share my story. I still actually can't believe I have my own book out. It has been a real pinch-me moment and I'm sure my English teachers at Italia Conti are stunned that I've managed to pull it off!

I really hope this book will help so many others going through grief and trauma. Thank you again for giving me this opportunity and allowing me to tell my story.

And finally a huge thank you to you, the reader.

Thank you for taking the time to read my story. I hope this book has given you the strength and power to know that you can tackle anything that life throws at you.

Acknowledgements

I hope it has taught you that when you suffer a loss, it isn't the end of your journey, but it can be the beginning of a new one.

Love and light always,
Kels x